GROWING IN FAITH WHEN A CATHOLIC MARRIAGE FAILS

For Divorced or Separated Catholics and Those Who Minister with Them

D1529143

GROWING IN FAITH WHEN A CATHOLIC MARRIAGE FAILS

For Divorced or Separated Catholics and Those Who Minister with Them

Antoinette Bosco

Resurrection Press
An Imprint of
CATHOLIC BOOK PUBLISHING CORP.
Totowa • New Jersey

First published in May, 2006 by
        Catholic Book Publishing/Resurrection Press
        77 West End Road
        Totowa, NJ 07512

ISBN 1-933066-04-0

Library of Congress Catalog Card Number: 2006923684

Cover design by Beth DeNapoli

Printed in the United States of America

1 2 3 4 5 6 7 8 9

I dedicate this book to my dearest friend, now in heaven, Cenacle Sister Thelma Hall, who first responded so enthusiastically to the importance of bringing the ministry of the Church to divorced and separated Catholics, and to Msgr. Dennis Regan, Msgr. John Alesandro, Msgr. Thomas Candreva and Father John Catoir, priests who understood our need not to be forgotten by the Church.

Contents

Foreword

L IKE Toni Bosco, I have written books for Catholics. And like Toni, I, too, experienced a divorce. When you're raised in the Church, and feel truly committed to it, divorce brings a special pain. Not only have you lost your personal dream of undying love in which you and your spouse pledge, "Grow old along with me, the best is yet to be;" but you may also feel—I know I did—that you have failed in your commitment to Church teachings. Didn't we all learn that marriage is one of the seven sacraments, intended to last "until death do us part"? I've never known a divorced Catholic who didn't try everything possible to save his or her marriage. But "death" can apply to a relationship as well as to a person. It is a simple fact: not every marriage can (or should) be saved.

For many years, the Church's treatment of divorced Catholics caused many divorced Catholics to feel like "second-class" citizens. Unless we could manage the slow process of annulment, we faced a terrible dilemma: choosing between the Church we loved and a second marriage to someone we had come to love. Did divorce in the Church inevitably doom a faithful Catholic to live alone?

As she has in so many of her books, Toni brings her deep knowledge of Church law and processes and combines it with her personal experience to bring to you, the reader, empathetic and helpful information. What has changed in the Church regarding annulments? How do you acquire one? How do you hold onto your Catholic sensibilities if you cannot get an annulment and decide to remarry outside the Church? And—perhaps most helpful of all—how do you build a dynamic, faith-filled life if you don't remarry? Toni is living proof that living alone does not have to mean a lonely life. She brings hope and personal witness to the surprising ways divorce can lead to a new, strengthened faith; and I would add, to a life that is rich and invigorating.

Barbara Bartocci, Author and Speaker

Introduction

The Special Life and Faith Challenges Faced by
Divorced and Separated Catholics

THERE'S a day I vividly remember dating back some twenty years ago that I could only label as "a new experience." Coming from a large family, and being the single parent of seven children, all my years until that day had been spent in the midst of people. Now, only one son, a teenager, was still at home. But this was summer, and he had gone to visit his cousins who lived five hours away. For a few days, I was alone when I came home from work. It was a new experience for me to be in an empty, noise-less house.

I wandered from room to room, somewhat disoriented, unable to cope with the quiet or to decide how to spend my time even though I had much to do and there were many choices I could make. Worst of all, I suddenly visu-alized my coming years as an endless stream of bleak, boring, lonely days.

Being human, my first reaction was to think about the most logical solution in our society for loneliness—mar-riage. Yet, for me, a divorced Catholic, marriage present-ed a dilemma, a painful, difficult decision—a choice between a husband, or remaining in communion with the Church. I had never before considered remarriage and so I had not investigated seeking an annulment.

That lonely day I recalled a woman once expressing in pain, "I am one of those divorced Catholics who cannot get an annulment. And as I look at the years ahead, I do not see how I can make it alone. I want so much to have someone to share my life with, yet apparently God is asking something else of me. Is there solace for me anywhere?"

Her question had particular meaning for me. Like her, I was asking, "How can I face the rest of my life alone?"

The answer, of course, is that I couldn't. No one can. Each of us needs relationships, commitments, interactions, friendships and closeness with others. Without relationships, life is sterile and we put ourselves in danger of pathological loneliness. The need for relationships is universal. And the challenge of finding them is one which must be met not only by divorced persons, but also by the widowed, the young, the old—and yes, even the married.

Divorced Catholics, who cannot get an annulment, find themselves having to face honestly whether relationships, other than one involving marriage and sexual intimacy, will be enough to get them through life happily. That can be painful and difficult to answer.

Certainly it is no good to obey the Church if it is not by absolute personal choice, based upon one's own convictions that the Church's teaching is right. If we obey for any lesser reason, then obedience becomes blind and will probably backfire, turning the conforming Catholic into an angry person, or a helpless, powerless follower of authority. If people feel controlled or manipulated by the Church, and then they "obey," they are in danger of losing contact with themselves and their self-esteem. This condition is personally devastating.

The divorced Catholic who does not qualify for an annulment is in a most unusual position. We are the only Catholics who are being told by the Church that we must stay celibate and single for the rest of our lives or be excluded from the sacraments. Nuns were able to leave their vows and their Order and marry; priests may become laicized and marry. In such cases, Church discipline can be dispensed. Divorced Catholics are tied eternally to our made-for-life vows.

We can see this position as a trap, or as an unusual setting for a new kind of self-growth. On the positive side, we can accept this as an opportunity to make a conscious choice for being individuals capable of standing alone and taking responsibility for our lives, while buttressed by the experiences and support of the Church to help us find greater meaning in our lives.

But we can't make this choice unless we believe the Church is right in its teaching on divorce and remarriage, and unless we can see all our pain and loneliness as a potential source of religious and moral reward. We need our priests and bishops to minister to us with understanding and human concern for our difficult life situation.

I have learned much in my many years of living alone. I have rejoiced for so many good times and mourned for the terminally hard ones I have endured as the mother of three deceased sons. There are times when I still walk from room to room, feeling lonely or lost. But in all honesty, this is not because I am a divorced Catholic who chose to accept the Church's teachings on remarriage. Loneliness hits me—and people in all situations—because we are human.

I have learned the good side of loneliness-- that it is God's way of asking me to grow towards Him. There I have found meaning in my life by being committed to work and causes I believe in, and by accepting my life with its sufferings as a way to a fuller realization of my capacity to be bonded to others, to nature and the very Source of life. Staying single has not been a sterile life, but one which allowed me the freedom to expand my circle of loved ones, staying conscious always of the wonder of living.

I know I could visit any Catholic parish in the country and find hurting people, facing the end of their marriage. They are learning, as I have learned, that life doesn't come with built-in guarantees that all will be well at all times. They expected to live "happily ever after," but were catapulted into a new life situation they were completely unprepared for.

What I learned, and can share with others, is that we can find resources within ourselves that we never knew we possessed, personal powers given to us by God, which can, even though sometimes with difficulty, move us from our darkness to blossom in joy. We must ask our Church to work with us, helping us rebuild our lives in faith.

Antoinette Bosco
Spring 2006

1

An Unexpected Interview— and a Crucial Ministry Begins

"I do not have to understand everything, but I do have to be open to all that betrays God's presence. Faith signals to me that he is there, in that chance event, that meeting, that friend, that word, that coincidence, that loss, that drawback, that perfectly timed joy. He weaves our lives, each strand of our lives, and his hand knows why the threads go off in all directions."

—Leon-Joseph Cardinal Suenens

MOST of the eighty-two women and twelve men who arrived at the Long Island Cenacle Center for Spiritual Renewal on a cool Sunday in the fall of 1971 were vocally suspicious of what this meeting was all about.

But curiosity—and hope—had dragged them here, some as far a distance as seventy miles. The announcement attracting them, carried in *The Long Island Catholic*, the diocesan paper of the Rockville Centre Diocese, and the local "Pennysaver," an advertising circular, had read simply:

"The first program of its kind, planned specifically for divorced and separated Catholic men and women, will be held at the Cenacle . . . For reservations, or further information, call or write Sister Thelma Hall . . . "

As people arrived to register, their motives in coming ranged from disbelief—"I didn't think the church knew we existed"—to amazement: "Thank God the Church is finally recognizing *this problem.*"

This "problem" was, and still is, the anguishing one faced by everyone who, for whatever reason, has had to confront the tragic fact that their marriage is a shambles, and that separation or divorce is inevitable. For the 94 people who had come that day, the problem was even more severe. They were Catholics, bound by their Church and their faith to remain true to their marriage vows, even if the marriage was no more.

The meeting had come about because of an unexpected conversation I had had with Sister Thelma a few weeks earlier. I was then a reporter for *The Long Island Catholic* and often went to the Cenacle to talk to the Sisters and to pray in the chapel. That day I met with Sister Thelma and she told me the sisters were re-thinking their mission, focusing on whether the programs they were putting on were really offering the spiritual renewal they claimed one could find there. Sister Thelma, who had converted to the Catholic Church when she was 29, told me honestly she felt they needed to "evolve" so as to meet the challenging needs of people who weren't being reached "by old approaches."

Then she faced me, with her wonderful smile, and asked me if I knew of any group whose needs were not being met by the Church, and, if so, did I think the

Cenacle could offer a new and tailor-made program to help them. I think it took me exactly one second to respond. "Sister, there are, indeed, some people out there who feel neglected, or even thrown away by the Church. I would be one of them if I didn't work for the Church. I'm talking about divorced and separated Catholics."

I had hardly taken a breath before Sister Thelma responded with a resounding promise that she would do something about this, asking for my help. Before I left that day, she had already made plans for an initial program she would have the Cenacle offer on a Sunday afternoon. I was to be a speaker, and then later she confirmed that the Rev. Joseph Conrad of the Brooklyn Diocese's Marriage Tribunal would also speak, specifically on what would be involved in trying to get an annulment.

When the responses to the publicity about the day devoted to divorced and separated Catholics started coming in, Sister Thelma knew we had come up with something very important. As she told a reporter that day, "We assumed that divorced and separated Catholics often feel they are forgotten by the Church. From the first calls that came in, I'm afraid this assumption is all too true.

"Several divorced Catholics said they had children reaching the stage where they are to make First Communion, and they are confused and uneasy about their own role. All of those who called said they feel very lonely and alienated, and they are anxious to have some contact with others who are carrying the same burden. Hopefully," Sister went on, "out of this program, we may be able to develop some kind of fellowship group to meet monthly for spiritual reinforcement." She added specifically that she was also inviting clergy and religious, believing this kind of inclusion was essential for the work of the Church to be fruitful.

What we found as that program continued over the months was that most of the Catholics stated strongly that they did want to remain in good standing in the Church. Though divorced, they were searching to find what avenues were available to them within the Church to rebuild their personal and spiritual life. They also admitted honestly that they knew very little about the Church's then theological position on annulment and divorce. As one woman put it, "We need help in learning to live with our new and difficult life situation. We need an identity, not only to know who we are—but we need an identity within the Church."

One thing all divorced Catholics understood was that we had become the new minority in the Church, suffering the difficult life of being isolated, different, lonely, and usually financially poor, thus needing the strength and refreshment of the Church perhaps more than at any other time in our lives.

What many of us saw from those Cenacle meetings was that the Church had begun to see divorced Catholics not as an embarrassment, but as fellow Christians, and were willingly offering understanding, not judgment. So many of us were touched by the very human counsel we received from a young priest, Father Thomas Candreva, who held a doctorate in Canon Law and became the voluntary chaplain for the Cenacle program. He specifically emphasized the connection between the legitimately human and the spiritual elements in each life. "Divorced and separated Catholics are coping with a very difficult human situation. It is important to help you see that *not giving up on yourselves and having confidence in life are fundamental religious attitudes.*"

The fact that a priest could connect so humanly with them helped the people who came to speak openly about their pain. One woman spoke out, saying, "For a long time you're plagued with a nagging sense of failure. Even when you know that there was no real marriage— because the relationship never developed at all—you can't help being overwhelmed at times with the feelings of tragedy. Something that should have grown and blossomed, shriveled up and died. That's a kind of failure. That's hard to accept."

The voices kept going—"A widow has a period of mourning and all her friends share this time with her. A separated woman has a mourning time, too, but you do it alone."

"What you think at first is loneliness turns out to be aloneness. There's a difference. Loneliness is a condition. It can change. Aloneness is the situation itself. It can't change. It has to be dealt with, and sublimated. Because you know that without an annulment you'll never be able to develop a male-female relationship of any significance as long as you want to stay in the Church."

"I get overwhelmed at times with the thought—who really cares about me? I have to battle against self-pity. I tell myself that self-pity is really hard anger gone underground and I try to fight it—because I know from experience that if it gets too far down inside me, I hit depression. That's like visiting death. God spare me from depression."

"In the course of a day you might be coping with stopped-up plumbing, all the ordinary household work like washing, cooking and cleaning, the demands of a job, transporting kids to the dentist or to music lessons, counseling a child with a school problem, being patient with a four-year-old who wants a green spoon instead of a red spoon, and maybe caring for a kid with flu. That's when some well-meaning friend calls and tells you, 'you don't have it so bad . . . ' "

The men and women who came to these gatherings openly questioned any priests who showed up, usually asking sincere questions, and sometimes difficult ones, like this: "A divorce is a destruction of something. Yet, if a Catholic woman thinks of marriage as a relationship where growth takes place, to become a 'oneness of life'—where this marriage becomes a secular witness to the sacred in this life—and then this growth never happens, was there really a marriage in the first place?"

What started to become clear as the months went on, and publicity about this program escalated, was that divorced Catholics had been given hope that the Church knew they existed, as one man put it. We soon got the word that a priest in Boston, the late Father James J. Young, had begun a group for divorced Catholics in that city. By 1980, his organization, called the National Association of Divorced and Separated Catholics (NADSC), and based at the Paulist Center, claimed 700 such groups were operating in 32 dioceses, with full-time directors of ministry to divorced people appointed by their bishops.

Father Young had begun his program after several recently divorced women contacted him, asking if he would arrange a series of lectures on the problem of divorce and remarriage. He did, and the series led to the founding of an on-going support group that became the prototype for many similar groups both in this country and in Canada.

Father Young wanted to end negative attitudes that divorced Catholics said they continually encountered. His own statement was—"The Catholic Church in this country has always been very pastoral, very close to people. The upsurge in divorce has brought this problem home for the first time, and it made us question the traditional attitudes which were very condemnatory.

"We've come to realize that, increasingly, this ministry and its efforts to help these people in their suffering in no way compromises our belief in the permanence of marriage. Rather, it shows us to be a compassionate people, and this makes our traditional values more attractive."

Father Young never wavered in his belief that divorced Catholics had not rejected the Christian value of the permanence and indissolubility of marriage. "In fact," he pointed out, "they wished they had achieved it and they perceived its power and beauty all the more for its loss . . . They yearned to be part of the Catholic community; they wanted acceptance and reconciliation."

As the '70s went on, it became clear that the Church was giving full recognition to the fact that divorced Catholics existed, and that we wanted to remain part of our Church. We needed respect and recognition from our parishes, not criticism and judgment. Now and then I would read about another new program in a story carried in a Catholic paper. Programs like "Stella Maris," begun by a priest in the Chicago Chancery Office, specifically in an effort to help Catholic divorced and separated women discover "who they are" were encouraging to me. The divorced and separated Catholic women going to Stella Maris had placed themselves under the care of Mary, "Star of the Sea," as they tried to help one another learn how to live a full and positive life as a person concerned with her responsibilities to God, Church, children and community.

The priest, the Very Rev. J.I. Cardiff, who was encouraging them released a statement about the primary purpose of Stella Maris, which we applauded back on Long Island:

"The divorced Catholic woman who, by her religious belief, is not free to remarry feels alone in the Catholic as well as the secular world. Hence, she feels security in the solidarity of a group of women who live as she must. She is able to accept the fact of her divorce and go forward to a positive and happy life. The group helps not so much by direct group therapy as by the mutual encouragement, individual aid and the example of other divorced women who are living happy lives. It is a group whose concern is not a backward look to the past, but a forward look to the future.

"Our purpose is not to counsel married women who might want help with marital problems. Nor would we attempt to counsel married women who want advice about whether to secure a divorce.

"The apostolic purpose of Stella Maris is to assist other divorced or separated women to adjust to their new status and to find fulfillment as women and Catholics within the framework of their status as divorced women. It reminds them that the graces of the sacrament of matrimony are still present to help them live without their husbands and to raise their children as children of God."

By the mid-1970s, those of us who worked in parishes or for the Church in other matters had become aware of the fact that a crucial ministry had begun, opening new doors to welcome divorced and separated Catholics who wanted to remain connected to the Church of their baptism. And many of us were aware that the question of annulments was being aired by theologians.

This was an area of theology that was of crucial importance to divorced Catholics, and remains so, to this day.

Questions for Reflection and Discussion

1. Have you wrestled with self-pity, depression or loneliness, and if so, how did you deal with this?

2. Did you talk to a priest about your marriage problems and, if so, how did he receive and counsel you?

3. In *Catholic New York*, under Support Groups, 14 are listed for Widows and Widowers, and only one for Separated and Divorced. Did you feel you needed a Support Group, and if so, did you find one, and were you helped?

2

How Divorce Emerged in the '60s as a Pastoral Dilemma in the Church

"I believe that in any trial or tribulation God will give us all the power we need to withstand it. But he does not give it in advance, lest we rely on ourselves alone If we trust in him we can overcome all anxiety for the future."
—Dietrich Bonhoeffer

"Earth has no sorrow that Heaven cannot heal."
—Thomas More

IN 1962, a truly great man named Msgr. Richard Hanley founded a diocesan newspaper to be called *The Long Island Catholic* for the new Rockville Centre Diocese which had been originally part of the Brooklyn Diocese. I was already a writer, mainly for the Catholic Press at that time, and through a fortuitous introduction, was introduced to the impressive monsignor, who promptly hired me to be his "Women's Editor." He made it clear that this was to be a "Vatican II paper," which appealed to me, and it didn't take too long before I convinced him to drop that "Women's Editor" thing. I didn't want to be a reporter in a box.

In all honesty, I was amazed that Dick Hanley—as everyone called him—hired me, for I was a mother of six children, all quite young except for my older son, adopted when he was 15. What he didn't know was that my marriage was a shambles, but I was faithful to it because it was a Catholic marriage. I had often gone to confession, or to see a priest, begging for some help with an impossible situation. But I would always be told that this was "God's will" for me, and was criticized because I had not accepted that "men had rights and women had responsibilities." It was 1960 before a priest at a retreat listened to me, getting me to really talk about my abusive situation, including how my husband even considered it my responsibility to financially support the household. He shook his head and commented, "You are living in such disorder, few people would stay sane." Thank you, Father.

But divorce was the furthest thing from my mind. I had a Catholic marriage, and I could not for a moment contemplate taking any action that would jeopardize my standing in the Church. And then, there were the children. I needed to be a good example to them, and fidelity to one's marriage, which could, indeed, mean hiding abuse, was crucial for maintaining at least the illusion of having a good Catholic family.

Unexpectedly, I started to hear many stories from other Catholic mothers as I would be invited as "the Women's Editor" to go to different parishes or events, covering these for stories in *The Long Island Catholic* paper. I saw a mother crying on the day her child received his First Communion, and asked her, "If Communion is so wonderful, why don't you ever receive Communion?" She told me she fell into a "no-man's land called remarried, divorced Catholics, and therefore cut-off from the sacraments."

Her story was sad. She had had a brief, unhappy marriage at age 17 that ended six months later. But it was binding. She found singlehood for life intolerable and so, when a good man came into her life, she married him in a civil ceremony. This gave her a new conflict—how to live as a Catholic, which was her heritage, while at the same time being judged by many as "living in sin." She said when her son asked her why she didn't receive Communion, the honest answer would have been to tell him "because the Church considers me a sinner," but she couldn't get those words out of her mouth.

As I went into more parishes, meeting with women involved in the whole range of societies doing good work for their Church and parish schools, I met too many who were once married and now alone, expressing heartbreak, loneliness, anger and confusion about what they saw as their desolate futures if they chose to stay in the Church, remaining ever-single.

There were people like Amy, who was 16, a junior in high school, when she found herself pregnant. The father was a boy, 17. "I know I was wrong to have sex with him," she told me, and then just shrugged. The families insisted that they marry, insisting also on the blessing of the Church. The teenagers were separated even before the baby was born. Amy said she saw a bleak future for both of them, living either as "single" for the rest of their lives, or entering an invalid union as a remarried, divorced Catholic, cut off permanently from the Church.

Grace started going to the Catholic Church, volunteering with the Altar Society, even though she was Episcopalian. She had been married in the Catholic Church to a Catholic man. He abandoned her after four months. There were no children from her brief marriage. Seven years later she fell in love with a Catholic widower who had four children. When I met her they had been married for five years, beautiful ones—except for the pain of being in an invalid union because of Grace's first, brief marriage.

Then I met Joan. She married the high school basketball star, a big wedding in white, nuptial Mass and all, two days after graduation. Three months later he went off to the Army, and three months after that wrote her a farewell letter. He came home long enough to get a divorce a few years later and then left the state. After eight years of loneliness, Joan met Ted. Soon, being mature enough now to know something about the realities of life and love, she wanted to marry Ted. The Diocesan Marriage Tribunal ruled hers a valid, consummated marriage, and said no to the possibility of an annulment, which, at that time was very hard for a Catholic to get.

All of these were true stories of human suffering faced by once-married Catholics who wanted to remain part of the community of the Church, but could do so only if they did not marry. They had learned a hard truth, that for a once-married Catholic, remarriage, not divorce, was the real cut-off from the Church. The explanation was painfully simple. Remarriage would place them technically in an adulterous union. The teaching was that when a Church sanctioned marriage takes place between two baptized Christians who freely consent to live with one another exclusively and for life, with a view to marital fulfillment in having children, and this pledge is sealed by physical intercourse, then this is a valid, consummated marriage. The bond is indissoluble; only the death of one of the partners could ever free the other to marry again.

I started to ask priests about this terrible problem so many remarried Catholics faced and the answers were most always the same: If the Church accepts remarried divorced Catholics into the full community, isn't this the first step towards weakening the doctrine of indissolubility of marriage? And what about scandal? Won't the good Catholics who haven't been sullied by some of the stickier problems of life be scandalized that the Church is now allowing "sinners" to have the same privileges as the unsullied?

Some of the priests I spoke with admitted that the question of how to counsel remarried Catholics who did not want to be cut off from the Church—but at the same time held to their belief that they had a right to remain in their present marriage as husband and wife, and not as "brother and sister"—was, they believed, one of the most crucial pastoral problems in the Church.

One young priest spelled out his own confusion and disturbance over this matter. "This year, at First Communion, we had eight sets of parents invalidly married because of a divorce somewhere in their past. They all considered their second marriage to be truly Christian and a valid union, but how could they prove this in a Church court? They seemed to be doing a fine job of raising their children within the Church and all they wanted was to receive Communion as a family.

"What could I tell them?" he asked, answering in the same breath, "I told them to follow their consciences."

At that time, while few clergy would agree with his "solution," all would have concurred that his dilemma did indeed point out the urgency of the pastoral problem. From the interviews and the research I began to do on the question of remarriage and annulments, I could see that both parish priests and bishops were genuinely concerned about the human suffering of Catholics caught in marriages that could not be saved, and for whom divorce was the only human option.

As for why so many marriages were ending in divorce by the '60s, studies by such respected researchers as the National Council on Family Relations indicated that people and the times had changed in a deep and complicated way. The role and education of women had begun to change drastically, with the emphasis on the man as the sole breadwinner also shifting. Perhaps most important, marriage had changed from being primarily a social relationship, mostly concerned with the nurturing of children, to being a very deep and personal relationship between man and woman.

With a new understanding of this changing relationship between the sexes, new questions were being raised: Are all people who marry really capable emotionally and psychologically of making a life-long commitment? Are some people actually unable to give or receive love, which makes them totally unable to enter a true love relationship?

Perhaps because it was the era of Vatican II, these questions were being considered by Church leaders, with new questions coming out from behind closed doors, asking— Can the Church's stand on divorce and remarriage be changed? Should Catholics who cannot save their marriages live the rest of their lives in implicit punishment, cut off from the sacraments if they choose remarriage in place of what for them would be the intolerable loneliness of enforced celibacy?

These questions were being tackled, significantly, by an increasing number of reputable theologians, canon lawyers, bishops, and priest-psychologists, all well respected for their sound thinking. The Rev. William W. Bassett, a Jesuit of the School of Canon Law at Catholic University of America, went so far as to proclaim that this issue of Catholic divorce and remarriage was being "aired in a context of pressing sociological, ecumenical and cultural needs."

Certainly, in the '60s, these Church thinkers were taking the problem very seriously. In fact, by 1970, Father Bassett listed in the *American Ecclesiastical Review* a partial bibliography of mainly post-Vatican II studies on the moral and canonical problems of divorce and remarriage in the Catholic Church, and it added up to six pages of fine print!

The new climate of discussion on divorce and remarriage erupted after an Egyptian Melkite Bishop brought the centuries-long buried issue up at the Vatican Council on October 29, 1965. Bishop Elias Zoghby challenged the rigid canonical discipline prohibiting remarriage after divorce. The following year, Bishop Francis Simmons of India was the first to startle many with the suggestion that the Church law on divorce might be changed, in an article on the Catholic Church and the New Morality in a late '66 issue of *Cross Currents*.

The year 1967 saw the real coming-out of the divorce-remarriage discussion, with a variety of viewpoints ventilated by knowledgeable churchmen on both sides of the Atlantic, starting that spring with a controversial book published by Herder and Herder, called *Divorce and Remarriage—Towards a New Catholic Teaching*. It was written by Msgr. Victor Pospishil, theologian, psychologist, canon lawyer, and one-time pastor, with 16 years experience as head of the Marriage Court for the Byzantine Rite Catholic Diocese of Philadelphia.

The Pospishil book stirred enormous interest and much criticism from reviewers who felt it was a neither-nor book—not scholarly enough to impress theologians, but far too scholarly for the ordinary layman.

I had the privilege of interviewing Msgr. Pospishil at his New York City apartment, and he told me plainly that he achieved what he set out to do—to get the divorce-remarriage impasse out into the open.

A few months later, at the annual meeting of the Catholic Theological Society of America held in Chicago that year, three papers were read on the subject of divorce, one of them by then world-known theologian Bruce Vawter. He brought out that the theology of divorce rooted in the New Testament has to be discussed from an understanding of the relationship of love and law in Christianity.

Father Vawter concluded his paper by indicating that the divorce question is certainly open to study and development. "Jesus' command regarding divorce was not the promulgation of a divine law, and obviously was never intended to serve as a model for the civil regulation of marriage," he wrote.

In August of that same year, Holland's famous Dominican, the Rev. Edward Schillebeeckx, got into the marriage-divorce discussion at a Toronto Theological Congress, emphasizing that the Catholic stand against divorce was not a hard and fast rule. "From the very beginning of Christianity, the rule of divorce has been subject to reinterpretation," he stated.

But they were also going beyond a discussion of law. They were talking about the "personal rights" of people to remarry; of the need for "mercy, not condemnation" in the pastoral care of divorced and remarried Catholics; the urgency to redefine "consummated marriage," broadening the then strictly biological definition to include "personal, psychic, and emotional consummation." Some came out and said that the canon laws on marriage had to be "brought in line with human needs."

Articles written by canon lawyers as the '60s were coming to a close pointed out some of the weakest points in at least four areas:

Legality—The question being asked was, who is more important—the person or the law? "Because our law has maintained a strictly legal basis for understanding the marital bond, we have institutionalized what in a real life situation can only be personalized," wrote the Rev. James R. Hertel.

Sacramentality—Can the fact of baptism really make a marriage automatically indissoluble? "The marriage law of the Church takes its form and structure from a theoretical and idealized account of the baptism event . . ." wrote the Rev. Leo M. Croghan.

What is the "bond"—Is it an external application, a juridical pronouncement? Or is it the mystery of a human relationship?

What is consummation?—Is it a physical act, or a growth together where individual egoisms are overcome by the dynamism of love so that a "synthesis of persons" results?

These questions could no longer be kept under wraps. The Jesuit magazine *America* devoted most of its February 17, 1968 issue to the subject of "The reform of canon law concerning marriage, annulment and divorce." While pointing out that they were not "endorsing" everything their writers were saying, the editors underscored they wanted to "draw the attention of our readers to an increasingly urgent problem in the life of the Church," being aired largely, they wrote, by canon lawyers.

Each discussion raised crucial questions, such as that asked by Father James R. Hertel—"Save the Bond or Save the Person?" He left little doubt that he had problems with the "law of the Church" that "looks first to the bond of matrimony, not to the parties who unite themselves in that bond." His position was that "A reassessment of the law that now favors the institution of marriage over the rights of the People of God should result in a new and enlightened law governing marriage."

Father Leo M. Croghan, then secretary of the marriage tribunal in Charleston, S.C. titled his discussion, "Is Baptism the Decisive Factor?" In a remarkably honest way, he pointed out the serious problem those who worked in marriage tribunals had to deal with because they were "still laboring under the old concept of baptism as a once-in-a-lifetime event that automatically binds a baptized person, whether he knows it or not, to the Church's discipline on marriage." He sought a reform of marriage laws to release the Church from being "still bound to an outdated, automatic identification of the union of two baptized persons with the sacrament of matrimony."

Father John Catoir, a doctor of Canon Law, who later served many years as the director of The Christophers' television program, saw the "tragic" situation of many "dedicated priests" who were "deeply frustrated by their inability to be of real help in cases that they intuitively know to be worthy." He then emphasized the "The mystery of human love is like the mystery of the universe itself, and canon law is only a tool . . . The law is designed to serve the common good, but the mission of Christ was to save individuals."

Rounding out these impressive positions in *America* was a discussion by a married couple, Louis Dupré, a philosophy professor at Georgetown University and his wife Constance, an attorney. They examined the issue of "indissolubility" of marriage rooted so far in the past. Pointing out that "A law always reflects the social and cultural conditions of the period that made it," they then asked, "Does the church's legislation on divorce sufficiently reflect the change in balance between the institutional and the individual aspects of marriage that has taken place in modern life? Is absolute indissolubility still the best way to protect the institution of marriage that has taken place in modern life?"

As the marriage/ divorce/remarriage discussion kept erupting in the post-Vatican II years, more and more respected theologians spoke out. Even the controversial area of incompatibility was being tackled. In *The Jurist*, July '69, Msgr. Stephen J. Kelleher, who had nearly a quarter century's experience in the marriage tribunal of the Archdiocese of New York, wrote: "The inability of two persons to enter or sustain marriage is often due to the deficiencies in one party which cannot be compensated and sometimes are aggravated by the other party."

Msgr. Kelleher concluded: "In our culture, the most stabilizing aspect of marriage is the fulfilled need of each party for the other . . . If it is acknowledged that the radical incompatibility of a couple—their relative incapacity to marry one another—is the causative factor in many unhappy marriages, the church will have to look beyond the present tribunal structure for a means of vindicating the rights of these people to remarry."

This was really new territory for theologians, and Msgr. Kelleher certainly was not alone in his courageous position. A few months after his article, *The Jurist*, January '70, carried one by the world famous theologian Bernard Haring who raised another explosive question. He asked, "Can the Church allow, or at least tolerate, a second marriage if a first, probably valid marriage, is destroyed?"

He offered the opinion, "Marriage is dissolved not only by physical death; it is destroyed—more than by physical death—by mental death, by civil death (like a lifelong prison sentence for one of the partners), and by the total moral death of a marriage."

With bluntness and compassion, Father Haring proposed: "The fundamental right of a person to marry should prevail against a thin probability regarding canonical validity of a destroyed marriage."

Clearly, the divorce-remarriage question had erupted into one of the hottest issues being examined in the '60s by a significant number of top theologians in the Church. They were re-investigating the Code of Canon Law sections that spelled out the conditions of indissolubility as regards Christian marriage, but also if and when remarriage after divorce could ever be permitted. By the end of the decade, the machinery and structure of the Church marriage courts had been vastly streamlined. Thus began a new era of breakthroughs in annulments. In increasing numbers, divorcing Catholics were going to the marriage tribunals in their dioceses, presenting their case, and hoping that the Church tribunal system would declare that their marriage was not canonically valid. Affirmative decisions were cause for celebration. An annulment meant becoming free, so one could marry again in the Church and receive the sacraments.

Questions for Reflection and Discussion

1. When and how did you know your marriage was in trouble?

2. Were you ever cut off from receiving the Eucharist because of an invalid marriage, and if so, how did you feel about it?

3. Did you and your spouse get any marriage counseling to help you deal with your problems, and if so, was this helpful? How?

3

What Theologians Were Saying about Divorce, Remarriage and Annulments in the Light of Vatican II

"God does not die on the day we cease to believe in a personal deity, but we die on the day when our lives cease to be illumined by the steady radiance, renewed daily, of a wonder, the source of which is beyond all reason."
—Dag Hammarskjold

"When we raise our hand to take God's hand, He does take our hand."
—James Pike

"Prayer does not change God, but changes him who prays."
—Soren Kierkegaard

BY the end of the 1960s, I had been divorced for two years, becoming a single parent with six children to continue raising and educating on my own. Because of my dedication to my Catholic faith, I had never intended to get a divorce, only a separation. My marriage had had an unusual start. It was an "arranged marriage." My father was a wonderful man, but a very strict Italian, who believed that a good father found a good man to be a husband for a daughter, and this had to happen before she was 20. I was 19, almost finished with my college studies, when, in conjunction with my grandfather, he found a man for me to marry.

I had told my father I didn't want to get married, but if he insisted, then he would have to find a good Catholic man for me. My grandfather, actually, was the one who found him, a neighbor of his in the city he lived in, a man who had studied to be a Jesuit priest, leaving after nine years. He saw my photo in my grandfather's house, and, strangely enough, agreed to marry me, all of this done, unbeknownst to me. After the arrangements were made, I was not permitted to be alone with him during the "courtship," but I was so busy with my college studies that it made no difference to me. I believed we would have a very holy marriage, after all, he had long studied to be a priest. I expected to have 12 children and I would name them all after the 12 apostles. That's how innocent, or stupid, whatever, I was back in 1948 at age 19.

I prefer not to go into detail about how difficult the marriage was, focusing rather on the joy God gave me in blessing me with seven great children. But from the beginning, I knew this union was anything but what a marriage should be. Yet, I was so devoted to my Church that I could not imagine ever ending this marriage, that is, not until I began to be honest enough to know nothing justified trying to raise children in a disordered household. By the mid-60s, at my insistence, my husband and I began going to Catholic Charities, seeing a marriage counselor. My husband spent the sessions telling this good man that I was the problem, there was nothing wrong with him.

By 1967, I had had it. I went to a lawyer seeking a separation. I still remember that warm Saturday afternoon in August when my husband was served with the papers. He was livid, but I reminded him that I had spent the past many years asking, begging, pleading with him to share the responsibilities of marriage and family. I had warned him that I would remove myself and the children from his disordered personality if he continued to show unwillingness to be healed. I don't think he believed I would take that drastic action. He stormed out of the house.

When he came back, I was in an old housedress, scrubbing the kitchen floor. He came into the kitchen, towering over me, his hands on his hips and with triumph in his voice, said "Father Canning (our pastor) wants to see you right away!"

I got up from the floor, took the car keys which he threw at me, got into the car, ignoring my dirty knees, drove to the rectory and knocked at the door. Oblivious to what kind of apparition I must have resembled, I asked for the pastor. I remained standing in the hallway. As Father Canning approached me, I blurted out, "I've listened to all the holy advice one can take for 19 years. The children and I are slipping into his disordered world. I won't let that happen. He's got to leave us alone. If God Himself came down from Heaven and said I had to continue to live with that man, I'd say, I'm sorry, but I won't. And that," I sputtered, "is the closest I've ever come to mortal sin in my life!"

My pastor, for whom I had worked in the parish long and well, led me to a chair. As I sat there, a 37-year-old woman, mother of six children still at home, my cheeks hot from surprise at my boldness, he said, "Antoinette, at first I thought your husband made some sense about how your problems had been caused by your interest in your job with *The Long Island Catholic,* and your refusal to accept his authority over the children. But then he talked *too long*! It became clear, he is a troubled man. I am recommending a good Catholic psychiatrist . . ."

The first visit to the psychiatrist our pastor recommended changed my life. After that fine professional interviewed both of us together and then privately, he berated me, giving me simple, strong advice. "Antoinette, what the hell's the matter with you? Get a divorce!"

Well, I had no intention of getting a divorce. I went for a separation. But I had a surprise coming. The good doctor ordered my husband to get a slew of psychiatric tests by the psychologist who, it so happened, worked for the diocese, doing these tests for people applying for annulments. To my surprise, he called me, telling me that I certainly qualified for an annulment, given the results of the tests he did on my husband.

This made me very interested in researching what was going on when it came to getting a Church annulment. I found that the Church had made two major breakthroughs in meeting the enormous problem of failed Catholic marriages. First, the machinery and structure of the Church marriage courts had been vastly streamlined in handling annulment petitions. But even more basic, the grounds for annulments had been greatly widened, based mainly on "a new understanding of what constitutes freedom and consent," two absolutely essential conditions for entering into a valid, sacramental marriage.

I interviewed the presiding judge of the diocesan tribunal in my diocese, who, at that time, was Father George Graham. He said, "The key phrase here is 'developing jurisprudence' in marriage cases, with canonists and psychiatrists, working together, particularly in the area of what constitutes an incapacity to make a valid marriage."

He went on, "We now know that there are many personality disorders which may not be psychosis, but which would, nevertheless, prevent one from fulfilling the conditions necessary for Christian marriage.

"In other words, the question we're now asking is, when are personality deficiencies serious enough to make it impossible for a person to fulfill a contract, particularly one of an intimate nature like marriage?

"This development of jurisprudence is where the real progress is being made," Father Graham emphasized.

An explanation of this term was expanded on by the Rev. Lawrence Wrenn in a work covering all the then possible conditions for annulments published in May 1970 by the Canon Law Society of America. "Canonical jurisprudence studies the recent contributions of related sciences like medicine and psychiatry, sifts them through juridic principles, and then, like the sea, gradually modifies the coastline of law," explained Father Wrenn. That took some reflecting, but it was very interesting.

I then interviewed Monsignor Marion J. Reinhardt, the administrative judge of the Brooklyn diocesan tribunal. He said that the breakthrough in the psychological area had made it possible for the courts to do "so much more for people" caught in a marriage broken because "their personalities drove them apart."

"We're finding that when a marriage breaks up, particularly in the early stages, one or the other had a personality disorder which interfered with their understanding of marriage and their freedom of will," Msgr. Reinhardt told me.

He stated further that a study of incompatibility done in his area gave overwhelming evidence to support the fact that some people who seemed to be perfectly normal on the surface, after psychological testing were found to have personality disorders which would have blocked their real ability to contract a valid Christian marriage.

Msgr. Reinhardt then affirmed that by working closely with psychiatrists and psychologists, and weighing the preponderance of evidence in each case, tribunal judges are able to determine with conviction when a marriage is null and void because of psychic and personality impediments. He then gave me some comparison figures to show me how this jurisprudence in marriage cases had developed in only the past four years. In 1966, the tribunal had made 12 annulment decisions, eight affirmative, four negative. In 1970, they made 95 decisions, 91 affirmative, and 4 negative.

Accounting also for this startling increase in marriage cases settled by this tribunal as the '70s began was the streamlining of procedures which went into effect on an experimental basis in July 1970 upon the direction of the U.S. Bishops. The major reform was in giving local diocesan courts the authority to handle most of the cases themselves without having to forward the case to Rome for a final decision.

Undoubtedly, by the 1970s, much progress had been made in annulments. But this caring priest pointed out that unsettling questions still remained about dissolubility of those marriages which have ceased to exist as growing relationships. Notably these would be cases where a spouse has been permanently deserted; or where a person no longer functions as a marriage partner, as for example, after an accident which has left one of the spouses irreversibly brain damaged and permanently confined.

"I've been trying to think through this question of dissolubility," Msgr. Reinhardt acknowledged. "Just as we today call some marriages null and void because they never truly came into existence, might we not at some future time call a marriage dissolved because it has ceased to exist?

"The big question is, what did Christ do? He made it incumbent that a couple shouldn't put each other aside. But," reflected Msgr. Reinhardt, who at that time had been a priest for thirty years, "if they are put aside by causes outside their control, what then?"

I raised this question with the Rev. Daniel Hamilton, who was then the director of the Long Island Diocese's Bureau of Information. He said, "What has to be made precise is—When does Christian marriage become indissoluble? This is the basic question." And he went on, "Canon lawyers and psychiatrists can raise questions, and these have to be taken seriously. But the ultimate judgment on what is an indissoluble marriage must come from the magisterium of the Church."

I now had more than adequate information about how far the Church had come in examining conditions that justified the granting of an annulment. I agreed with the Catholic psychologist who had tested my husband, telling

him that I did believe the conditions of my marriage justified an annulment. Yet, I also told him I had no intention
of going through that process, certainly not while I had
the full and total responsibility of raising and supporting
my beloved six, still young children. Yet, within a few
months, I was a divorced woman. My husband, involved
with a woman who wanted to get married, went to
Mexico and got a divorce. I wasn't a part of this at all,
didn't even have to sign a paper.

Perhaps from my own experience, and because I started to see so much sorrow at broken marriages, I became
extremely interested when a good Catholic couple,
Harriet and Ed Garzero, called me in the fall of 1968 asking if I wanted to write a story for *The Long Island Catholic*
about a marvelous experience they had just had making a
weekend Marriage Encounter. Founded by a Spanish
priest, Father Gabriel Calvo, this was a religious movement aimed at reviving the relationship between a husband and wife, and had only just been introduced in the
United States.

I did several stories about this great movement, also
having the privilege of interviewing Father Calvo. Then
Abbey Press asked me to write a book, which I did, called
Marriage Encounter, A Rediscovery of Love, which was published in 1972. What I didn't publicize was the pain I was
put through, when a priest and some couples who had
branched off from the original Marriage Encounter group,
openly derided me. They proclaimed that I, a divorced
woman, had no right to write about marriage.

When some problems started to develop with the
movement, I wrote a lead article for *The Long Island*

Catholic, entitled "The Pro's and Con's of Marriage Encounter." This so angered the priest in charge and a leading couple in the movement that they actually came to the editorial office of *The Long Island Catholic,* berating the priest-editor for letting me, a divorced woman, write about Marriage Encounter.

One of the stories that circulated was that I had disguised myself as a nun to infiltrate a Marriage Encounter weekend so as to get "inside information." And I got several phone calls from unidentified persons blasting me as an enemy of marriage who was trying to destroy Marriage Encounter.

Up until this time, I had known that prejudice against divorced women had always existed, but I never expected that it could be so vicious within the Catholic Church. I prayed from deep in my hurting heart that the work ahead that I would do could soften the hearts of those who had not had to endure the trauma of an ended marriage. Remarkably, the beginning of this healing came from the early members of Marriage Encounter, which itself had had a split within its ranks. The original members continued expressing great respect for me.

I was becoming ever more convinced that divorced Catholics, who remained faithful to our Church, had an important job to do. We had to let our brethren know we deserved respect. By this time, Sister Thelma Hall and I had been working several months with divorced and separated Catholics coming to the Sunday afternoon sessions at the Cenacle. Here I kept hearing so many sad stories of brutal criticism heaped on a person because their marriage had failed. But I also saw that what we were doing together was giving us hope that in time we would be accepted, not criticized, and perhaps even be given credit for trying to restore and rebuild our lives which had turned out so differently from what we had hoped for and expected. As one man said, we were finding here "a center where we can come to gain strength so that we can go out again and take up our lives refreshed."

Sister Thelma told me, "Month after month it becomes more evident that divorced and separated Catholics are searching for a place in the Church. So many have thanked me for bringing them together and making them feel at last that someone cares for them. Belonging to a program where Catholics in a similar situation can get together has helped them to sharpen their sense of identity in the Church and break through their feelings of inadequacy." Father Candreva's concern for us was also so evident, especially as he would point out the connection between the human and spiritual elements in the lives of each one of us.

From the beginning, we had been convinced that the people who were with us had come because they wanted to hold on and grow in their Catholic faith. Thus, at the Cenacle, each meeting was climaxed with a special liturgy which was truly the expression of love we all "hungered for," as I remembered a mother saying. She had been deserted by her husband and was a teacher in a Catholic elementary school, working to support her five children. I interviewed her, and still have her words, "I don't want to sound icky pious, but I need a relationship with God within the Christian community—which is my heritage—especially because human love was turned off in my life. I've been in and out of happy times with God, and I've learned endurance, which sometimes is as desperate as 'hang on, Suzy, He'll be around again!' These meetings have helped to keep a sense of His presence strong." And expressing the feelings of divorced and separated Catholics, she added—"Religion is not just for the more fortunate. It's for me, too."

Then, in the late '70s I got a call from Neil Klupfel, editor of *Today's Parish,* a fine magazine that had often carried my articles. Neil told me he was starting a book publishing business to be called Twenty-Third Publications, after the great Pope John XXIII. He asked me if I wanted to write a book for him. I hardly took a minute to think before I said, yes, a book on Catholic single parents. Neil said, "Go!"

The book came out in 1978 and received very affirmative reviews, with nice phrases, like "she writes with a wisdom that flowers from experience," "she is strong of spirit," and my favorite, "I like this lady. I like her book. I recommend it heartily."

I was unprepared for the calls that came into me from Church organizations, all wanting me to come to them to give a talk on being a divorced Catholic, raising a family alone, after this book came out. I went to as many as I could and still hold on to my job, which had been a position with the State University of New York at Stony Brook, Long Island, since 1972. Everywhere I went, I found good people, many with sad stories of their shattered marriages and huge responsibilities as single parents, but all of them, staying with the Church of their baptism, seeking help in growing in their faith. I truly believe we inspired one another.

Questions for Reflection and Discussion

1. Looking back, were you and your spouse mature enough to enter into a marriage relationship that would be good for life?

2. What was your understanding of what an annulment meant, and did you ask a priest to help you investigate your chances of being eligible for an annulment?

3. Did you want to be a part of a Church-based program to support separated and divorced Catholics, and if so, were there any that you joined?

4

How New Pastoral Concerns for Divorced Catholics Kept the Church Doors Open for Them

"Faith means putting one's hand in the hand of God with the certainty that God will not mislead him. Hence no conviction could be deeper, firmer, or more unshakable than that achieved by supernatural faith. . . . The Church is not a movement, but a meeting place; the trysting-place of all the truths of the world."

—Father John A. O'Brien

IN the summer of 1980, Father Dennis Regan, then rector of Immaculate Conception Seminary in the Diocese of Rockville Centre which was celebrating its 50th anniversary, arranged an unusual, high level conference which he called "Spiritualities for the '80s." His idea was that since this anniversary coincided with the start of a new decade, this would be a good time "to reflect on where we've been and where we're going." He wanted to have a "spiritual marathon," and so arranged for some twenty talks on issues that brought out "the spiritual thirst of people for Jesus Christ—the God-man—in their lives and the need to express this faith experience externally." In other words, his point was that one must seek for the God within and the God outside—the link between Word and world.

Much to my surprise, I got a call from Father Regan. He asked me if I would be one of the speakers, talking specifically on "Spirituality of the Divorced and Separated." Other speakers to be there included such well-known theologians and writers as Father Adrian van Kaam, Monika Hellwig, Father Basil Pennington, Father Matthew Fox and many others, with Leon Josef Cardinal Suenens of Belgium giving a final reflection.

I was overwhelmed, mostly because I felt we—that is, divorced and separated Catholics—had made such progress, that we were being recognized and given a voice in this very high level conference! I felt that the title alone was an acknowledgment that the experiences of our lives can truly be pathways to a new relationship with God—that they could be a dynamic, if painful, breakthrough to a deepened spirituality.

I said I would be honored to give a presentation. In the printed program Father Regan respectfully presented my talk to the bishops, clergy, religious and lay people. He noted that divorced and separated Catholics "often come together for mutual support and to minister to each other. However, sympathetic understanding is not enough. These persons seek tangible help by way of guidance and direction. Antoinette Bosco will share with us the ways and means she has discovered to cope with a life burdened with so many difficulties. Her experience will help us to see better ways we might assist these people in developing their spiritual lives."

Then I was in for a real surprise. I asked Father Regan who the audience would be. Besides priests and nuns who worked with lay people, he thought there would be as many as 100 or so bishops from different dioceses in the nation at the seminary for this conference. My contribution, he said, would be "to develop the threads or directions which would be unique to a person who finds him/her self separated or divorced." The thought of speaking to so many bishops was, I admit, rather intimidating, but I also believed it could be an opportunity to get high-level understanding for what divorced and separated Catholics were asking of our Church leaders. What I found that week was that many bishops, priests and nuns were very aware of the work divorced and separated Catholics had begun in hopes of opening the hearts of the hierarchy and fellow Catholics, seeking understanding and acceptance.

I never worked so hard in all my life in writing what turned out to be the honest cry from my heart to let Church leaders know the truth of the pain we live with when a Catholic marriage fails, and how we "grow up," leaving our old law-based faith behind, now holding on to our faith, redesigned, but in so many cases, stronger. In substance, this is what I told the bishops:

I began with the story of our pastor sending me and my ex-husband to that good, Catholic psychiatrist back in 1967, telling them how shocked I was when he told me I was a "masochist," pointing out that anyone who had lived 19 years accepting continued psychological abuse has to be someone who wanted to suffer. He forced me to examine not only my situation, but my religion.

I protested desperately that it was my belief in God, my religion, my spirituality that had given me the strength to bear the suffering. I reminded him that I was carrying my cross, that I had been living up to my spoken marriage vows, accepting their promise that when the "sacrifice is complete, the love would then be perfect." I even quoted Bishop Fulton J. Sheen who spoke of pain and hard times on his syndicated television show of the early '50s. He said we suffered because good is to come from it, and he gave an example, pointing out that the marble had to be chiseled and pounded before it became a Pieta, and that metal had to be burned and subdued before it could be molded into a beautiful shape. That was my spiritual approach to life that had gotten me through some 30–plus years.

I related how the psychiatrist interrupted me, no doubt to get me off my pulpit, asking "Why isn't this kind of spirituality working any more? Are you coming to your senses, maybe growing up? Are you beginning to recognize that it is dishonest to accept a pathological situation while comforting yourself that you are being holy by doing this?"

The bluntness of his questions startled me, I had been suppressing them so long. That session marked the beginning of my new spiritual growth, thanks to that Catholic psychiatrist who helped me understand what was destructive in my own personality that had prevented me from growing in my understanding of true spirituality. He suggested that maybe I was still stuck in the messages of my strict Italian father and mother that translated "obey, obey, don't question, don't ask, obey!"

He guided me to learn that if being spiritual means anything at all, it is to be living in a state of harmony with yourself, with others and with God. There's nothing "holy" about remaining in some infantile state of "obedience" by hanging on to childishly understood doctrines and advice, using this as your excuse for remaining in an intolerable situation which ultimately becomes destructive to your spiritual maturity. I also had to learn, and believe, that after divorce, there could be a rebirth ahead, one that would release a new spiritual energy leading to personal harmony and peace.

Within a few weeks on a Saturday morning in October I received the decision from a Family Court judge about my petition for a separation. He granted the separation, but ruled that since there wasn't enough money to support two households, my husband could continue living in the house. I found this astounding, and frightening. I called that good Catholic psychiatrist immediately, asking for helpful advice on what to do. He responded right away. "What the hell are you calling me for? What are YOU going to do about this?"

I got off the phone, infuriated. I kept asking myself those questions over and over, and finally I understood. That good psychiatrist wasn't being mean to me. He was trying to get me to accept the fact that the time had come when I—that is, ME, in big letters—had to make the decisions that were right for me. No longer could I turn my problems over to someone else, not a priest, not a family member, not a counselor or even a psychiatrist. Building a new life was my problem, my responsibility, and no one else's.

I made a decision then and there. If, as the judge ruled, my husband could live in our house, then I and the children would move out. That Saturday morning, I went out and, scraping together every penny I could, found a place to rent, big enough for me and six children. On Monday morning, I had a moving van take just the furniture I would need for myself and the children and we left our family home. Our new life had begun. It wouldn't be easy, but I knew it would be better.

I related my story to the bishops that afternoon at the seminary, and then told them how incredibly painful it is to accept that after divorce our lives have been thoroughly altered and there's no going back. We are in pain and mourning because we have experienced the death of beautiful expectations. There is no emptiness like the one that emerges at the grave of a relationship which pledged to make you become one with another, living permanently as "two in one flesh."

Even when divorce is a relief, because it signals the end of a destructive relationship, it still puts our lives into disarray. We are dissected, divided. We are at a point where we are most vulnerable to desolation and despair. Most of us experience incredible difficulties during this early period, especially if we are left with the job of raising the children. When you are so immersed in problems, incessant work, daily confrontations with prejudices and other assorted pains, you come dangerously close to asking, with Jesus, "My God, My God, why have You forsaken me?" The spiritual turmoil gets expressed in other questions, too. You wonder, if God is a loving God, why has he let my life become so bleak, so lonely? Faith itself becomes elusive and you often feel abandoned by God and the Church.

I frankly think this collision head-on with the "moment of truth" about one's relationship with God is almost universally experienced by people who undergo a crisis of extreme intensity. It can be divorce, the death of a loved one, an attack upon the physical body by illness, accident, war, depression, alcoholism, being the victim of a crime, being parents of a child who flaunts the law, or commits suicide, maybe even the shock of confronting one's own limitations. Traumas such as this can shake you to your very roots so that sometimes you're even asking the rock bottom questions, like—What is this existence all about anyway? Who needs it? Who wants it?

If we've been trained in a religious tradition, when we get to this point we usually experience the shock of learning rather suddenly that old religious clichés don't work any more. When you are in a new, threatening place, you need a deeper understanding of what your relationship with God can become, or neither religion nor spirituality make sense.

I remember my feelings that day when I left the rectory as being determined to survive, but near despair. What I had really told my pastor was that I was no longer looking for religious pat answers to help me in my crisis. I had translated the "accept it" answers I had gotten from too many priests in the previous years into immobility. I had, in effect, poured holy water over a destructive situation, and all this had done was freeze me into spiritual retardation, a rigid rule follower. When I had come to the point of "enough!"—expressing this as I had to my pastor—I had taken the first step toward healthy spiritual freedom, and I was terrified.

I remember thinking about a story I had read in a magazine by the late writer Mary McCarthy. It was about her days in a convent school when, on a lark to get attention, she had decided to tell the sisters and a priest-chaplain that she had "lost" her faith. Before the static was over, a strange thing happened to her. She had, indeed, lost her faith. The story ended with her leaving the school, feeling as she had years earlier when she was just learning to swim, discovering way out in the deep water that her water wings were floating way behind her.

That's how I felt then. I was inexperienced, in water over my head and I had lost my water wings, the security of my childish faith. Still, I did emerge from each of the depths into which I had been plunged. Each agony brought me closer to recognizing that my divorce which was a severance from a human relationship was parallel to the pain of being disconnected from God. Divorce made me yearn for the miracle of reconnection, the gift of being able to pick up the pieces of a shattered life and build a new order.

Each struggle led me to a place where I had not been before. I was rediscovering little by little, pain by pain, what it was that God wanted me to learn. At this time, I was constantly reminded of an analogy given by Father Hans Kung when I had the good fortune many years earlier of learning from him at a five-day theology conference. He was speaking on the need for re-interpretation of Scripture, explaining that this did not imply that anything new was being added to the original message. Rather, it was more that the original message was still being discovered.

Father Kung likened this to walking into a darkened room and turning on a lamp. The area around the lamp would be disclosed to you and you could believe that you now had seen everything in that room. But suppose another light went on, disclosing yet some other furnishings in that room. Your knowledge and vision would then be greatly broadened because you now had more information about that room.

I often thought of what he said and felt that divorced and separated Catholics are in a position where the darkened corners of themselves come to light with many surprises. One thing I found was that I had little patience with pat answers that are supposed to say something profound about the difficulties of your life. Most times people don't know how to react to us, especially in the early days after divorce, and so they tend to cover their ignorance by giving you nice and easy God-talk. I never again wanted to hear "put everything into God's hands," or the worst, "God sends suffering to those he loves most." I felt that this kind of talk trivialized spirituality.

A darkened corner of my life that came to light as I was rebuilding our lives after the divorce was seeing anew how our journey to God is over rough territory. He gave us life and wants us eventually to be with him forever. But in between, we put on the coffee, make the bread, give birth to the children, deal with our conflicts and struggle for internal peace. Divorced and separated persons need words of substance and assurance with clout that we can cement the pieces of our lives together and without bitterness towards God or any human being trust ourselves, believing that we will win our struggle to regain wholeness once more. Rather than "carry your cross," as I was so often told to do by a priest, I would say, "love your life because it came from God; stop beating yourself with your failure-strap; and seek a professional counselor for help with your serious here-and-now problems."

Then, of course, there is the loneliness, that searing emptiness that comes after the loss of a relationship, which has a two-pronged potential—spiritual devastation or triumph. When loneliness is extreme, it is perhaps the most cruel pain we can experience because it is caused by a descent into isolation, in which we feel cut off from every other entity, living and non-living, and moreso, even from ourselves. Extreme loneliness is the horrendous state of being out of touch, existing nowhere, conscious of being totally disconnected from all that gives meaning to life and desperately yearning to escape from this terror.

Divorced and separated persons are especially vulnerable to the negative aspects of loneliness. You run the danger, at times on a recurring basis, of visualizing the years ahead as an endless stream of bleak, boring days, thinking no one else knows loneliness as you do. You find yourself wondering, "How can I face the rest of my life alone?"

The answer is, of course, you can't. No one can. Each of us needs relationships, commitments, interactions, friendships and closeness with others. The need for relationships is universal. Without relationships, life is sterile and we put ourselves in danger of pathological loneliness. The mistake we must avoid is believing that anyone else can bestow happiness on us. Each of has to find our own individual way of coping with and moving out of loneliness.

As the years went on, out of my struggle and with prayer, I came to understand that my very life had become truly an expression of my new-found faith. Faith is a response to God's signals, which very often are more like shocks jolting us out of the comfortable positions we'd much prefer. I was responding to a daily challenge to face the realities of my life, good and bad. Even when God seemed out of the picture, somehow I knew I was still hanging on to him for dear life. Faith was truly the activator in my life, because it was faith which motivated me to run a house and feed a big family on the proverbial shoestring; it was faith which helped me work so hard, without giving up; it was faith which made me see the beauty and joy in my life instead of concentrating on the bleakness.

Without faith, I would not have been plugged into purpose. I would have lost the sense that life has meaning, and that somehow I fit into the whole scenario that started when God—as he told Job—laid the cornerstone of the Universe. Gratefully, I had learned that the judgmental, punishing God I was introduced to in my past rigid religious training was not a God I related to when my life was in disarray. The lonely, suffering Jesus came to my rescue in my daily living, becoming my role model for faith, as he showed all of us that our existence, as our loving Father designed it, was to be about fidelity to love and goodness.

All that I have just said was, in essence, what I also presented to the bishops at that great convocation at the seminary on Long Island. I could never have anticipated their reaction, but it was a tremendous surprise. The bishops, and all there, clapped and then rose, giving me a standing ovation. I was humbled, almost to tears, with gratitude that these tremendous people had evidently related so well to the words coming from my heart.

Several of the bishops spoke to me later in the break period, and told me they were going to go back to their dioceses and start a ministry for the divorced and separated, and for single-parent families. Many groups for divorced and separated Catholics had emerged by the late '70s, providing a place of acceptance, spiritual help, moral support and practical advice. But this was not yet a really flourishing ministry. It gave me joy to read in the next few years that in many dioceses bishops had officiated at "healing Masses" for divorced Catholics, reaffirming the Church's concern for its troubled members.

After my single parenting book came out, I met with many Catholics who had suffered the trauma of divorce. Yet, I could see that divorced persons who had strong religious beliefs found their religion to be—not an obstacle—but a support, as I had. I found a study by secular researchers Drs. Kenneth Kressel and Morton Deutsch that actually backed this up. They wrote:

"Because divorce is such a central experience, an individual's religious affiliations are more likely to be maintained and even strengthened when the experience is conceptualized within a religious framework. Thus, clergy may reassure clients regarding their standing in the religious community and encourage them to maintain religious ties.

"At a deeper level, clients may be encouraged to see their emotional suffering and personal doubts as a potential source of religious and moral reward," they affirmed.

I never expected to get so many calls for help from Catholics with failed marriages as I did when more and more I became known as the "friend" of divorced and separated Catholics. It was sad to see that while much progress had been made, with many dioceses now accepting us, somehow the parishes were still ignoring us. I remember a call I got from a long-time friend who coordinated a religious education program for her parish of some 3,500 families. They had just finished doing an informal census to get a data-profile of the individuals and families in the parish. They felt this would be a useful tool in helping them set up new programs for the coming year.

But a funny thing happened on the way to the countdown. With uncomfortable regularity, families kept cropping up with a missing dimension—a parent. By the time the census results were calculated, the workers had discovered that nearly thirty percent of the families in the parish were headed by a single parent. My friend called me to ask if I would be willing to lead a program, give a talk, or do something that would let these families know they had been noticed.

The parish leaders were frankly shocked. They hadn't realized that divorce, separation, death and family abandonment had so infiltrated and changed the family-profile of a long-standing Catholic parish.

I spoke out in talks and through my syndicated column that people in special situations, like divorced Catholics, single parents, gays, the disabled, prisoners, immigrants need a ministry that fits them here and now. You can't reshape the people. It's the ministry that needed to be reshaped.

I had a tremendously heartwarming invitation as we approached the '80s, when the late Bishop John McGann, of the Rockville Centre Diocese invited me to be one of his four lay representatives to the annual conference of bishops of the eight dioceses of New York state. The family, being assaulted by many different pressures was the theme of the conference, held in Albany that year. Where could families turn for help if not the Church? The fact that I was invited by my bishop to represent him was most significant, for I was divorced and a single parent. The invitation was a clear and underscored recognition that the Church in my diocese was ready not only to accept divorced and separated Catholics, but also indicated that the Church was saying it had something to learn from us.

A major insight that came out of the conference was the need to shape parishes into true extended families, beginning with a reeducation process to eliminate a language barrier when the word "family" is spoken. Most then, as even now, agreed that "family" still connoted the idea of father-mother-children. But if the Church was going to work seriously at making the parish into a "family," then "family" had to be redefined to include all people in all situations.

A point stressed throughout the conference was that families urgently needed a sense of hope, and that only we, individual families united through our parish membership into an extended family, could give this hope to one another.

It was a remarkable privilege to spend two days with the bishops of my state, sharing lunch and liturgies, getting to know some of them on a personal basis and, above all, feeling their intense concern for their people. This was an experience that, especially as a divorced Catholic and single mother, truly recharged my spiritual batteries and revived my confidence in our bishops. I was wishing that every divorced Catholic who wanted to grow in faith could have been there, too.

Since then, thank God, the word has gotten around that we exist in large numbers. But more has still to be done to give recognition and acceptance to us. Many churches have groups for teenagers, married couples, senior citizens, and sometimes for single adults and widows and widowers. But rarely can we find a parish group for divorced and separated Catholics. I think I know the reason, for as one pastor told me he feared such a group would become a "singles party," leading to invalid marriages.

If sometimes we still feel like the ignored Catholics in the parish, we should not take this lightly. We have voices and we can change this by participating in the work of the Church, both within our parishes or our dioceses. Our life has been altered, and that's all the more reason why it's up to us to let the Church know that we want to grow stronger in our faith, and that we need help at every level.

Questions for Reflection and Discussion

1. How was your Catholic faith "redesigned" by divorce?

2. Did divorce open a pathway for you to have a new relationship with God, and if so, how?

3. If there were times when you felt forsaken by God, what did you do to reestablish your relationship with him?

5

The Most Serious Spiritual Decision a Divorced Catholic Faces—to Remarry without an Annulment

"Faith is to believe what we do not see, and the reward of this faith is to see what we believe." —St. Augustine

"You have shown me many afflictions and hardships
but you will once again revive me.
From the depths of the earth
you will once again raise me up.
You will restore my honor
and console me once again." —Psalm 71:20-21

WHILE I would doubt if there are Catholics today who are completely in the dark about the fact that the Church does grant annulments, many in failed Catholic marriages are unfamiliar with the exact meaning of this process until they actually get to the Marriage Tribunal Office in their dioceses.

A good explanation of annulments is given in the *Encyclopedia of Catholicism*, edited by Father Richard P. McBrien:

"**Annulment**, a declaration by a church tribunal system that a marriage was not canonically valid. Perhaps the first thing to be noted about this definition is not so much what it says as what it does not say. It does not, for example, say that an annulment indicates that a relationship, even a loving relationship, never existed between the parties. More importantly, it does not even say that a marriage never existed between the parties, but only that that marriage was not a canonically valid one . And finally, an annulment does not say that children born of an invalid marriage are illegitimate.

"A marriage may be invalid according to the Church for one of two reasons: because of a law, or because of a consent that was in some way defective . . ."

It's that last phrase that has caused much confusion. Some Catholics believe that all kinds of games can be played to try to prove "defective consent." Still some others go so far as to believe that Church annulments actually can be interpreted as officials saying a Christian marriage can be a "temporary arrangement."

Nothing could be further from the truth.

I have never known any priests or divorced and separated Catholics who believe that the bond of a true marriage can be broken. And moreso, all of us hold firmly to the declaration of Jesus, that when two people, fully capable of making a permanent union, are joined by God in marriage, such a union could not be dissolved.

The real area where the search for truth is crucial in the marriage situation rests in the four words, "whoever God joins together." That's been the long misunderstood phrase that used to be interpreted legalistically, not realistically. Now, for the past several decades, the definition of Christian marriage has no longer been the old cut and dry equation that—consent, plus consummation, equals Christian marriage.

New ingredients from progress both in theology and the behavioral sciences led to a shake-up of that equation. Among these have been the development of a marriage theology which sees the covenant, that is, the mature love bond between people, as an essential ingredient before two people can call their union a Christian marriage; and then, scientific progress has been made in understanding the psychology and emotional make-up of people, that can determine if and when a person is capable of entering into a Christian marriage. Finally, one has to have a spiritual base, a faith commitment to Jesus, before that person can enter a Christian marriage. God cannot join two people forever in matrimony if one of them does not believe in God or his Son.

All of these developments have led, not to a change in the doctrine of indissolubility of Christian marriage, but rather, to a change in defining what constitutes a Christian marriage.

A new condition was added to the old definition of Christian marriage. The Church now says—Consent, plus consummation, plus the *capability* of these two persons to enter into a lifelong, mature relationship involving mutual love and shared responsibilities, plus spiritual values—these are the ingredients of a Christian marriage.

Once the Church began looking at Christian marriage with this new vision that focused on the living, growing relationship of two people, as well as the legal contract, "broken marriage" could be reexamined. The Church no longer shunted these aside as "hopeless" situations. The Church, with compassion and wisdom, could then ask, Were these two people capable of making vows requiring maturity, or at least the potential for maturing? Was this ever a Christian marriage in the first place? When their judgment came up negative, then it could be seen that a Christian marriage never truly existed here, freeing the Catholics involved to put aside their past pain and start fresh. As one Catholic friend told me, with happy tears, after her annulment came through, this was her "superlative welcome home."

The story for Catholics who did not, and do not, qualify for a Church annulment, has a very different, and a very sad ending. If they marry again, they are judged to be in a state of mortal sin and are thus forbidden to receive the Eucharist. The Pontifical Council for the Family at its 13th plenary assembly in the Vatican in 1997 published "The Pastoral Care of the Divorced and Remarried." While there was an acknowledgment that "The Church is extremely sensitive to the sorrow of her members," the Council urged Bishops to "help the divorced who have been left alone to be faithful to the sacrament of their marriage," but also to "invite the divorced involved in a new union to recognize their irregular situation which involves a state of sin, and ask God for the grace of their conversion."

The problem of second marriages that are judged to be invalid because of a first, Catholic marriage that was judged to be valid, has long presented problems for Catholic theologians. Writing in the *Jurist*, January 1979, the Rev. Anthony Kosnik explained that certainly, "failure to conform to canonical discipline regarding marriage cannot always be identified with loss of faith. It would be a travesty of his pastoral duty if a priest simply dismissed all people involved in marriages that are canonically invalid as sinners against the law of God and excluded them from the community of the faithful. This would be an unwarranted identification of canonical legislation with the will of God."

This pastoral problem was clearly stated in an article by Jesuit Father Richard A. McCormick in *Theological Studies*, March 1971: "Should those who are involved in a second marriage after a valid and sacramental first marriage be admitted to, or be encouraged to receive, the sacraments? If so, on what grounds? If not, why not?"

By 1972, a committee of the Catholic Theological Society of America (CTSA) was set up specifically to study the problem of second marriages. Mainly they wanted to consider the problem of how remarried, divorced Catholics could participate in "the full life of the Church," especially since "a shift in emphasis has taken place in Catholic thought on the nature of marriage."

"Before Vatican II, the emphasis was on marriage as a contract," they wrote. "Marital consent was aimed at the act of sexual intercourse and primarily at the procreative aspect of this act. Since Vatican II the Church sees marriage and marital consent oriented not simply to a particular act but to a total community of life and love . . . In cases where this kind of community has never developed, we believe that there is reason to question the validity of the original consent . . ."

The theologians went on, "In our judgment the absolute prohibition of a second union in cases of doubt is not a necessary public protection of Christian marriage." And, again, "It is the judgment of this committee that a marriage case is not automatically closed by a negative decision in the legal forum."

Then the CTSA committee boldly stated, "Most of those presently living in invalid marriages have been deprived of integral participation in the life of the Christian community. It is the judgment of this committee that, whatever may have been its theological justification or benefits in the past, there is serious reason to modify this practice."

I did a lot of interviews with theologians back in the early '70s when Sister Thelma Hall and I were running the programs for divorced and separated Catholics, many on this crucial issue of what kind of connection could a remarried, divorced Catholic have with the Church. Father Dennis Regan, a moral theologian on the faculty of the major seminary on Long Island, pointed out something very important. He said, "Reception of the Eucharist is not a reward for goodness, but the means by which we remain in a relationship with Christ. And it is necessary for people in ambiguous situations to remain in a relationship with Christ."

Father Regan went on, "We must remain aware that law has built-in limitations. Church law cannot envision every individual instance and situation. There has to be an opening for people who know a truth even though this cannot be proven under the forms of legal structure."

Because of these very serious questions being raised by theologians concerned about too closely linking canonical legislation with the will of God, we started to hear a new phrase, the "internal forum." What this meant was simple enough to explain: Church law maintained that a canonically valid marriage was unbreakable—that was the "external forum." But if remarried, divorced Catholics truly and honestly believed in their conscience that they were now free of the previous marriage bond, then they could receive the Eucharist—that was the "internal forum."

The internal forum solution, then and now, shakes up not only many a priest and theologian, but also many a parish Catholic, who may be scandalized if couples known to be in second (invalid) marriages are seen receiving the Eucharist. Early popularity of the "internal forum solution" brought back the old notion of "scandal" into the writings and discussions of the pastoral approach to remarried Catholics. Jesuit Father McCormick suggested in his articles that a commission be appointed to study this pastoral problem, emphasizing the theological reasons for any and all conclusions they may then propose.

"Otherwise," he stated, "there is the danger that individuals will go their own way, solving difficult, practical problems off shaky theological premises or destructive sentimentalism."

All the questions being raised emphasized how seriously the American bishops were taking the question of failed Catholic marriages. Yet, by the end of the 1970s, fears were being raised in some conservative quarters of the Vatican that the American Church was granting too many annulments. Figures released by Vatican officials in 1980 showed that 31,000 annulments had been granted by U.S. tribunals in 1979, compared to 445 in 1968.

At this time, a 74-member commission of bishops completed a work begun 18 years earlier, requested by Pope John XXIII, to draft a new code of canon law that would replace one that was published back in 1917 and reflect some of the changes occurring after the Second Vatican Council of 1962-65. One of the changes redefined the procedure and grounds for granting marriage annulments.

By late 1981, the commission approved a new code of canon law that formally recognized "severe psychological immaturity" as grounds for approving an annulment. It stated, "Incapable of contracting matrimony are those who are (1) affected by a serious illness or psychological disturbance, (2) have a serious defect in their ability to understand the reciprocal rights and duties of matrimony."

By writing the psychological grounds into canon law, the Vatican Commission guaranteed that every tribunal had to recognize this as a basis for annulment. This was a true breakthrough because, as the Rev. Daniel F. Hoye, then associate general secretary of the National Council of Catholic Bishops, explained, acceptance of the psychological grounds into the code for the universal Church was "an affirmation of what we've always said here in the United States, and would be consistent with the jurisprudence practices in the highest courts of the Church."

Yet, the very year that saw this new canon law approval for annulments on psychological grounds, also saw a strengthening of the "traditional response, that when divorce occurs in a consummated marriage between two baptized persons, and one or other of whom remarries, then the right to the Eucharist has been forfeited . . . This theological stance is based on the notion that Christians in such a second union are living in a permanent state of sin; they are also imperfect symbols of what the marriages of Christians should signify," explained Theodore Davy, who heads the pastoral theology department at the University of London, writing in "Modern Catholicism, Vatican II and After" (edited by Adrien Hastings).

He goes on, "The 1980 Synod of Bishops on marriage and family life debated this issue, but was unable to reach any pastoral conclusions. And when Pope John Paul II issued his exhortation on marriage and the family in 1981, *Familiaris Consortio,* he too felt unable to change the traditional stance, saying of the divorced and remarried, 'Their state and condition of life are objectively opposed to that union of love between Christ and the Church that is signified by the Eucharist . . .' "

Professor Davy adds that a "careful reading" of the late pope's document, however, "gives one reason to conclude that Pope John Paul II was not closing the pastoral debate, but was stating that the theological arguments had not yet been "sufficiently clarified," and that "we are in the midst of a development that has not reached its final goal yet."

Then, the British professor, who worked many years with the Church's marriage tribunals raised an interesting point about what he calls the "scandal argument" when it comes to divorced Catholics remarrying without benefit of annulment. Couldn't it be that "the scandal the community is receiving at present is caused by the exclusion of people from the Eucharist, and not by their reception?" he asks, adding, "The argument that the divorced and remarried are imperfect symbols is disquieting, if for no other reason than because in a Church all of whose members are sinners, it must lead then to a further question, 'Who then can be admitted to the Eucharist?'"

While the point Professor Davy raises can lead to important and interesting theological discussions, it does not help divorced Catholics remarried without benefit of an annulment move closer to getting re-attached to the Church they love. The official word has not changed. As a document available on the internet, written by someone identified only as "a Pennsylvania Bishop on Marriage" and provided "courtesy of the Eternal Word Television Network" states: "In reference to divorced Catholics only those who have received an ecclesiastical declaration of nullity of a previous marriage or whose former partner is deceased are free to marry in the church and to participate fully in her life."

The document underscores that "the use of the so-called 'internal forum solution' for cases of divorced and remarried persons who are personally convinced that their previous marriage was invalid is unacceptable, unnecessary and pastorally unsound . . . the 'internal forum solution' has the effect of ratifying an erroneous judgment of conscience against the reality of objective moral truth . . . The ratification of erroneous judgment of conscience obscures the demand for moral truth . . . True conversion of heart and growth in holiness are thus hindered since the person sees no need to repent, reform and grow in the spiritual life . . .

"Second, the 'internal forum solution' undermines the teaching of the Lord and the church on the indissolubility of marriage and the sanctity of sexual union . . .

"Third, we are concerned about the problem of scandal
. . . The more serious danger of scandal is that in witness-
ing such situations others will be confused, weakened
and misled into immoral behavior themselves. . . . If the
Church were to allow this practice it would itself become
a participant in the trends of our society that undermine
the stability of marriage and family life."

Clearly, the annulment question is one that increasingly remains actively important to all Catholics, from bishops, canonists and laypersons, to the pope. In early 2005,
a new Vatican instruction on annulments, titled *Dignitas
Connubii* was issued at a Vatican news conference. John
Allen, Jr., reporter with the Vatican, explained, "The purpose of the document is to provide a step-by-step guide
for judges in processing requests for annulment, applying
the Code of Canon Law adopted in 1983, in light of the
experience of the intervening 23 years." He said that in
general "the instruction gives more power to judges to
short-circuit procedural appeals that have the effect of
unnecessarily slowing down the process . . . The aim of
the document was to avoid pointless delays and objec-
tions, but at the same time to ensure that the outcome is
not automatic, and that a serious judicial process is
observed."

A few months later, at a meeting on July 25, 2005 with
some 140 priests, religious and deacons, Pope Benedict
XVI spoke about the pain of divorced and civilly remarried Catholics, saying, "Given these people's situation of
suffering, it must be studied . . . None of us has a ready-
made solution . . . each person's situation is different."
America, the Jesuit magazine, then reported: "Pope Bene-

dict said that Catholics must keep two things in mind: first that even if divorced and civilly remarried Catholics cannot receive the Eucharist, they are part of the church and are loved by Christ; and second, that suffering out of love for God and for the church is 'a noble suffering.' While participating at Mass without receiving Communion is not optimal, he said, 'it is not nothing; it is involvement in the mystery of the cross and the resurrection of Christ.'"

Just a few months earlier, in late February, *America* magazine had run an article titled "The Anguish of Annulment, A Personal Journey," followed two months later with an astounding number of letters prompted by this piece. The writer of the first article, requesting anonymity, wanted to tell of the pain he, his wife, a divorced Catholic, her former husband, her mother and especially her children went through because of the annulment process, which regurgitates so much of the past both from the parties involved and those listed as witnesses to their marriage and subsequent situation.

The letters published two months later were, with a couple of exceptions, also tales of difficult and painful experiences in undergoing the annulment process. As one woman wrote, "Much of what was revealed would have been better left behind us and our families. Truth may have been served; charity was not."

A priest, ordained 49 years earlier, pointed out that the annulment process "costs the U.S. church millions each year. Annulments are simply not affordable in poor countries . . . Insisting that only an annulment can dissolve a Catholic marriage has caused the greatest attrition in the

U.S. Catholic Church in our era . . ." And other letters confirmed this, by telling of annulments not granted.

At least one letter spoke of the annulment process as being "a tremendous benefit in seeing the relationship as it really was and knowing things I would do differently if I ever married again. It brought great healing to me and, I believe, to my ex-husband, and I truly felt very loved and affirmed by everyone I dealt with through the entire process. It renewed my faith to the point that if the annulment had been denied, I would have accepted that judgment and moved on with my life alone. Fifteen years later, I met a wonderful Catholic man, and we were married after a two-year courtship, unmarred by any ties to the past. "

When the 21st Synod of Bishops was held in Rome in late October 2005, it was dedicated to the theme of the Eucharist. As reported by Rome correspondent John Allen, two topics considered by some to be "taboo" were raised, one of celibacy for priests, and the other Communion for divorced Catholics remarried without getting an annulment. Bishop Luis Antonio G. Tagle of Imus, Philippines, said, "In the absence of the priest, there is no Eucharist. We should face squarely the issue of shortage of priests." And Archbishop John Atcherley Dew of Wellington in New Zealand, brought up the remarriage issue:

"Our church would be enriched if we were able to invite dedicated Catholics, currently excluded from the Eucharist to return to the Lord's Table. There are those whose marriages ended in sadness; they have never abandoned the church, but are currently excluded from the Eucharist."

But at the close of the Synod, Catholic News Service reported what Cardinal Alfonso Lopez Trujillo, president of the Pontifical Council for the Family, had to say—and it was this: the fact that civilly remarried divorced Catholics may not receive Communion "is not disputed or disputable."

"They are in an objective situation that goes against the will of God and does not permit them to receive Communion," said the Cardinal, who then went on to criticize the media for giving the impression that "this was an open question, as if doors were open for the future, creating expectations for a possible change."

Yet, "the problem of the divorced and remarried is very much a burning question," countered German Cardinal Walter Kasper, president of the Pontifical Council for Promoting Christian Unity. Then he underscored, "Every bishop in the Western countries knows this is a serious problem, so *I cannot imagine the discussion is closed.*"

Parish priests I speak to tell me they too feel the pain of the exclusion felt by civilly remarried divorced Catholics who want and need to be sacramentally united to their Church. They send these couples to their diocesan marriage tribunals to apply for annulments, giving them all the positive information they can put together, along with encouragement, and then they do the only thing they can—they pray.

Questions for Reflection and Discussion

1. Did you investigate getting an annulment, and if not, why not?

2. Do you understand and agree with the Church's official position on annulments?
3. What would be your position on the validity of the "internal forum" (conscience) when it comes to receiving the Eucharist?

6

When Divorce Creates a
New You—Now, a Single Parent

*"The fullness of life does not come from things outside us.
We ourselves must create the beauty in which we live."*
—Poet, C.E. Cowman

I HAVE often thought back to the year 1971 when I was asked by the planners of a Religious Education Congress in my diocese to give a workshop on Catholic Broken Families. Since I was a divorced Catholic, raising six children, then from ages 8 to 21, they thought I would be ideal as a speaker for this topic.

My first reaction was that religious education leaders had finally come around to recognize that Catholic broken families existed. But my second reaction was swifter and stronger. That was *my* family they were referring to. My family—a broken family?

I examined the premise. "Broken" means disrupted—and clearly a new single parent family is a disrupted one—but it also means to be cut up, displaced, not whole. I had known some broken families: places where an alcoholic parent kept the children in a tortured prison of inconsistency, loving them one minute, beating them the next; places where the livid anger of two parents was so deadly that children escaped from them by developing their own angry behavior, often getting into drugs; places where a parent alone had taken on a new prospective partner, so disruptive to the household that the children had to be taken away and placed in foster homes.

On the other hand, what was a whole family? A place where there is a sense of unity and peace; where all the members of the family feel comfortable; where they care for each other, would go to bat for each other, and would never deliberately hurt one another. That was the kind of home I had—not a broken family, but a whole one.

I responded to the invitation to participate in the Religious Education Congress by telling them, yes, I'd do the workshop, but only if the title were changed, from Catholic Broken Families to Catholic One-Parent Families, giving them my reasons for insisting on the change. They agreed, with apologies and enthusiasm.

I think I had learned at that time, from my personal life and from giving talks to many Catholic women's groups in Long Island parishes, meeting divorced mothers like myself, that little focus had been placed on how divorce had "recreated" us. No longer were we wife and mother. Now we were Catholic single parents—and soon I learned that this included some fathers, too,—who, with little history or current attention to guide us, fell into this new identity.

I learned from my own situation, and from the single parents I met and worked with, that the place where we had to start redefining ourselves was to see our wholeness by strongly fighting the "broken family" image that plagues every family with a missing parent. Why did our families have to be judged according to external images? It was clear to me that a family must be defined by its essence, by the atmosphere which permeates it, by the reality of the relationships of the members.

But it was also clear to me just how enormous a job it was for the newly single parent to maintain—or often rebuild—a family unit where all could live together in that mutual place called home in peace, harmony and productiveness. For the custodial parent alone, as I knew from my own life, was left with all the problems, crises, work and responsibilities of family life, without the support and nourishment of marriage.

And children of divorce have so many needs and rights: they need to be fed physically, emotionally, and spiritually; they need to be understood, to be treated with patience; they need to be protected from the by-products of their parents' one-time marriage so that they can be free enough to cope with their own burden of growing; they need to be young, to be disciplined, to be educated, to be given opportunities for creativity. The needs of children fill books, and meeting these is more than a job for two parents. How can a parent handle that burden alone?

Catholic single parents coming to our group meetings at the Cenacle monastery on Long Island used to ask me that last question a lot. I would take a deep breath, pull out my sense of humor and answer, "With difficulty, great difficulty!"

In the past three decades I have done considerable research on the effect of divorce on families, Catholic and of other faiths, or no faith at all. I saw much depression when a marriage break-up was due to a spouse walking out to start a new relationship with another person.

Mary, a neighbor, was one friend I tried to help when her husband walked out and moved to a different state with another woman, leaving her to complete the job of raising three children, ages 11 to 15, with little income. The first sign of his desertion of the family was the exterior of the house, with grass overgrown, shrubs untrimmed and the wood shingles badly in need of a painting. I visited her one day when she was distraught and depressed, feeling out of control because her two sons had been having a fight over a game of chess.

"Everything in my life is chaos," she said, sweeping her arms around the room. "Look at the broken chairs, the leaky washing machine and the holes in the rug. We had beans and rice again for dinner. Toni," she said, her eyes filling with tears," I'm not making it—not financially and not emotionally."

I understood her anger. It was caused by the sense of being unfairly abandoned by husband and God, and left trapped in a situation she couldn't leave. She was also falling into depression, that terrible disability that saps one's energy, one's vision, one's caring about self, others and life itself. When a parent is in this disabled state, there is a spillover effect which settles like gloom over a family. The family becomes joyless and is in trouble.

The more I got involved with divorced and separated parents, the more I got to understand one truth—no one was going to appear like a fairy godmother and solve our problems; only one person could do what had to be done to make a difference and bring health back to the family and that was—*ourselves.*

What's needed first, of course, is to begin healing the terrible wounds that most often result from abandonment and divorce. These affect both women and men who are the deserted spouses. Healing is not at all easy. So often I wished I had a magic wand that could bring peace and happiness regardless of the pains in life one is subjected to. That, of course, is a fairy tale. Healing oneself is probably the hardest work one can undertake, and I had learned, and would tell other divorced people, it was not something one could really do all by oneself.

By the late 1970s I had become known in Catholic circles as being a Catholic single mother because of my book, *A Parent Alone.* I was contacted by many diocesan groups that had begun programs for divorced and separated Catholics, thanks to the national spotlight that had been turned on by Father Young's work, with the dedicated co-worker Sister Paula Ripple, emphasizing the need for a ministry to help us and keep us connected to the Church. I would most always be asked to talk on the parenting-alone aspect of divorce. But then, the deeper pain, and sometimes tears, would start to show as my brother and sister Catholics told me that while they appreciated the new parish efforts to help them, they still felt abandoned by the Church.

I heard many a sad story about a parish incident that the teller would say could only be interpreted as rejection by the Catholic Church. One woman, with tears, related how she was asked by her pastor to resign as a religion teacher after her husband left her and obtained a divorce.

The pastor put on a very kind face and told her he thought she'd be uncomfortable teaching in the religious education program when she herself had a "broken family."

At that time I had just read a book called *Creative Divorce*, where author Mel Krantzler quoted a woman saying: "The other day I was at the store and spotted the mother of one of Jimmy's classmates, whom I had gotten to know through the PTA. She actually ducked behind a display of gardening equipment to avoid having to talk to me. It's getting to be a pattern. This town is like Noah's Ark. If you aren't part of a pair, they shut you out."

That motivated me to write one of my syndicated columns on the dishonesty of calling one-parent families "broken," and I received several "thank-you" letters, like this one from a woman in Illinois: "I can vividly remember overhearing two nuns talking about my sister and me—'they are such nice girls and do well in school even though they're from a broken family.' I didn't know my family was broken. My mother had somehow managed to convey a positive image of our family to us. You seem to be doing the same. God bless you!"

I did a lot of hugging those days, sharing pain with single mothers, assuring them that their families were not "broken" and that in time, the Catholic Church would accept us; sheer numbers indicated this would have to happen.

Somewhat slowly, parish support groups for divorced and separated Catholics began to crop up. I worked with newly single mothers, trying to convince them they had to find the "power source" that would force them to believe they could, themselves, trigger a change in their lives that would bring healing and new life to their families. Often, it was seeking out a support group such as newly formed Divorced and Separated Catholics groups, or Parents Without Partners; or taking an adult education course to learn new skills that could help her get a needed job that was the first step to healing. In cases where a newly single mother was too depressed to turn herself around by her own efforts, I would try to help her understand she should seek professional help, in the same way that anyone seeks medical help for bodily illnesses. All too many of these mothers had no idea they could go to Catholic Charities and get help, that they didn't have to suffer through a disabling period alone.

Some divorced parents told me they had too much pride to ask for help. I would respond, from experience, that the help needed was temporary, and the caring people in these places were professionals whose goals were to help them and their families regain optimism and independence. I would say, look at me. I, too, had to accept the fact that my life had been thoroughly altered, completely different from what I had expected it would be for a Catholic wife and mother, and there was no going back— because there was no "back" to return to.

A major change for all single parents is seeing and accepting how the structure of the household, too, changes because the management style is different basically from that in a two-parent family. I soon found, personally, that single parents have a different relationship with their children, marked by a direct line of relationship between parent and child—mutual dependence, partnership, greater equality in allocation of chores, and considerable "negotiation." The father-mother head, with its hierarchical patterns, does not exist in single parent families. Nor can we ignore what I called the larger, existential questions of life and love, purpose and destiny within the context of the single parent situation. The job of single parenting isn't just big, it's huge and monumental!

Yet, I had always had what I called "heavenly help," and that was my strong religious beliefs in the love and goodness of God which became my support. Sometimes I found that very hurting Catholics, still in deep pain, had moved away from believing that religion could be a real help for them. But even a secular study of escalating divorce in the '70s by Drs. Kenneth Kressel and Morton Deutsch backed up my belief. They found that "because divorce is such a central experience, an individual's religious affiliations are more likely to be maintained and even strengthened when the experience is conceptualized within a religious framework. Thus, clergy may reassure clients regarding their standing in the religious community and encourage them to maintain religious ties." And then they added something astounding, making them sound almost like theologians: "At a deeper level, clients may be encouraged to see their emotional suffering and personal doubts as a potential source of religious and moral reward."

I know it takes a while after a marriage begins to "explode," ending in divorce, to get to a place of peace and healing. The pain of a broken marriage is universal, because it is the death of beautiful expectations. There is no emptiness like the one that emerges at the grave of a relationship, especially the relationship which pledged to make you become one with another, living permanently as the marriage vows say, "two in one flesh."

But to stay in that state of emptiness is the continuation of violation to self and family. I truly learned there is an individual and a communal responsibility for a family disabled by divorce to find help and healing, and join what I am brave enough to call "the living" again. Sooner or later we have to admit that we have to rebuild our lives within this new single situation. We have to find new self-direction—and that's a task requiring a great deal of self-awareness, self-understanding and honesty.

The honesty is especially important when there are children involved. I read many studies on children of divorce in my years as a single parent. I had to admit that most children of divorce definitely suffer the effects of loss—losing one live-in-parent, often the loss of a familiar home setting, a neighborhood, security and even, in a way, their former identity. They are now a different, an altered, family and so often they see, or at least feel themselves as being changed in an undefined way. When I was researching my single parenting book, I came across a study by a psychologist and a social worker that found virtually all children under age five showed distinct distress symptoms after their parents' divorce. Many showed more aggressive behavior, irritability, whining and crying. But the report went on to say something very important for single parents to focus on:

"Follow-up studies done a year after the divorce showed that the symptoms tended to disappear in two-thirds of the group if the parent who remained with the youngster offered adequate physical and loving care. This held true no matter how strong the initial reaction to the separation."

But what about the other one-third? The professionals went on. "But a third of the children continued to be openly troubled. Further investigation revealed that in these cases the intensity of adult emotions surrounding the divorce has not diminished. These children lived with mothers [or fathers] who still felt hurt, humiliated and angry with their former spouses."

This study pointed out something every one of us who are single parents get to know—that no matter how necessary a divorce may be—and it is often the only solution for an impossible marriage situation—one fact remains indisputable: divorce exacts a price in the social and emotional growth of children. The challenge every single parent faces is to be determined that you will respect your childrens' right to good parenting, work hard to achieve this and pray hard that the trauma they experience, whatever the degree, is temporary.

Research on the effects of divorce on children goes on continually. In November 2005, the *New York Times* reported on a national survey of 1,500 respondents, ages 18 to 35, half with divorced parents and half with married parents. Higher numbers of those with divorced parents checked off these statements: "At times I felt like an outsider in my home; I felt like a different person with each of my parents; It was stressful in my family; I always felt like an adult even when I was a little kid; I had to take sides in my parents' conflicts; Sometimes I felt like I didn't have a home; I was alone a lot as a child."

Children with married parents checked off—"Children were at the center of my family; I generally felt emotionally safe."

The source for this survey was said to be research by Elizabeth Marquardt and Norval D. Glenn, scholars with the Institute of American Values, "a nonpartisan advocacy group that strongly emphasizes marriage," according to the *Times*. Ms. Marquardt, author of a recent book, *Between Two Worlds*, was quoted to say, "All the happy talk about divorce is designed to reassure parents. But it's not the truth for children. Even a good divorce restructures children's childhoods and leaves them traveling between two distinct worlds. It becomes their job, not their parents' to make sense of those two worlds."

The *New York Times* reported, "There are no reliable national statistics on divorce, but most experts say that even with divorce rates edging down, about three quarters of a million American children see their parents divorce each year. The new survey, based on the first nationally representative sample of young adults, highlights the many ways that divorce shapes the emotional tenor of childhood."

Reading this rather negative account of the effect of divorce on children reminded me of a book that came out in the early 1980s titled *Children of Divorce* by two California psychologists, Judith Wallerstein and Joan Kelly. They had interviewed sixty couples right after the break-up and then again five years later. They reported that five years after the break-up, 34 percent of the children were happy and thriving, 29 percent were doing reasonably well, but 37 percent were depressed.

Reading their findings more carefully, I also found that within five years 76 percent of the adults involved had remarried, and 11.6 percent of the remarried ones had gotten a second divorce. That meant that a majority of the children had to deal with a stepparent and with a new disruption. They had to make serious adjustments on both the emotional and physical levels in a short period of time. No wonder so many were depressed.

Yet, it is never wise to jump to conclusions when reading research results. For every negative result on the effects of divorce, another study can come up positive. When I would get someone coming to one of my talks on single parenting to chastise us, inferring we could not be good parents if we were divorced, I would pull out a quote from a book by a Harvard sociologist, Dr. Robert Weis. His research showed that single parents placed a great value on the creation of intact families although, admittedly, in a new structure. Single parents display a "determined devotion"—that was his phrase—to their children. "Raising their children successfully--providing them with care, protecting them from danger, trying to ensure that their homes are happy—tends to become for single parents their most important goal."

"Life is filled with trade-offs, and I worry that it's so easy to slip from descriptions of problems to one-size-fits-all prescription. There will always be couples who need divorces," said Stephanie Coontz, a historian and author of *Marriage, a History*, responding to the Marquardt study. She, like many other researchers, points out that most children of divorced parents grow into successful adults, even as they acknowledge "that the process is difficult for them."

After the *New York Times* published the article on the Marquardt study and poll, a number of readers sent in letters, all very understanding of the pain of troubled marriages. As one woman wrote, "If you were to ask older children about their parents' divorces, many would say they wished that their parents had divorced sooner, emphasizing that it's better to be *from* a broken home than *in* one," as put by reader Carol Silverman.

Again, I always emphasize what I see as a tremendous difference between single parenting and a "broken" family. We single parents were put into a lifestyle with tremendous burdens, but with a great potential for gaining new strengths, new unities. We find ourselves forming a new family structure of what an intact family can be when there is only one parent. The new situation causes many changed relationships within the family. We have to accept realistically what's good and what's bad about our new situation. And we have to accept the fact that our self-image is changed, but that doesn't mean it's bad, it can be a much improved self-image over what one had in their marriage.

The courage we show in building a new life in spite of what can be a very painful time means we are actually people who are successfully solving our problems instead of remaining frozen and immobilized in our problems. Ahead, there can be a rebirth into peace, because now we're looking at life in terms of its gifts instead of its deprivations. And here is where we find God.

I have learned that our families are Christian families as truly as any two-parent, intact family. With Christ as the Center, where values of love, justice, goodness and generosity prevail among the members and these values are willingly extended to others, our families should rightly be acknowledged as Christian families.

Questions for Reflection and Discussion

1. How would you describe your "new identity" after divorce when you became a single parent? Did you find prejudices that, though unspoken, were there, sometimes making you defensive?
2. What did you find to be the most difficult aspects of your new job as a single parent?
3. What efforts did you make to keep yours a Christian family?

7

The Many Surprising Ways Divorce Can Lead One to a New, Strengthened Faith

"Faith in God is faith in some ultimate unity of life, in some final comprehensive purpose which holds all the various, and frequently contradictory, realms of coherence and meaning together."   —Reinhold Niebuhr

IN early 2005 I was asked by leaders of the North American Conference of Separated and Divorced Catholics if I would give a keynote talk at their annual international conference that would be held at the end of June. Irene Varley, former executive director of this organization, founded in the fall of 1975, contacted me, telling me that the theme of the gathering that year would be "Celebrating the Journey from Darkness to Joy." She asked for my ideas on this, and, thinking of my many years as a divorced Catholic, mother of seven—three sons deceased—and grandmother of 15, I responded:

Life doesn't come with built-in guarantees that all will be well at all times. From expecting to live "happily ever after," we can be catapulted into a new life situation that we were com-

pletely unprepared for. Yet, surprisingly, we can find ourselves calling upon resources we never knew we possessed, and that is the beginning of a new and challenging journey. If we can believe we have personal powers given to us by our God, we can, even though sometimes with difficulty, move from our darkness to blossom in joy.

To go forward in the face of overwhelming odds—which is all too often the situation of a once-married person—is to risk failure, true. But to make progress on our life's journey, we must take risks, or we will never learn, feel, change, grow or love. This is what I have learned in my lifetime. I chose to leave a marriage, becoming the sole parent and financial supporter of six of my seven children, then ages 3 to 16—my older adopted son was already a Navy veteran and married—because it was the right choice. I put my trust in Jesus to be my teacher, my confidant and my companion.

And now three-and-a-half decades later, I can testify to how the Lord helped me come through the darkness, to know his bright joy. He never gave me false assurances that life would be easy. On the contrary, he allowed me to be put on the cross many times over, but never to the death, always soothing my wounds with a bouquet of joy.

In all honesty, I rarely received the specific agenda I requested. But I learned that while we don't "receive" what we specifically ask for, what we do get is tailor-made help from God to get us through whatever it is we're facing. Like it or not, Jesus helped me understand and accept that his Father's plan was not to fix things for us but to get us to fix our lives and the world ourselves.

I prepared my talk wanting to share what I had honestly learned from my life, that no matter how difficult and painful our experiences may be, because of my gift of baptism, my faith, which linked me to the Lord Jesus, I never felt abandoned, or in despair.

Funny how things turn out sometimes in life. I never got to that Conference. I sat twenty hours in an airport due to problems the airline company said were out of their control. But in that time and since, I made new friends and learned a lot more about NACSDC and how this organization has worked to strengthen the faith of Catholics whose marriages failed.

Bob Dulinski of Hancock, Michigan, former President and now Office Manager of NACSDC, shared his personal story with me, a beautiful account of how divorce led him from being a man of little faith to finding God again. Raised Catholic, but not feeling particularly attached to the Church, he was married in 1978 in a Lutheran Church. "Our married life was not a spiritual one. We were both from alcoholic families so we didn't have the tools to make a marriage work," he said

By 1991, parents of a young son, they were separated, followed by a divorce in 1993. "I floated around, didn't have any good relationships, getting rejected because of lousy choices. You try to bury pain with a lot of things—alcohol, sex, credit cards, relationships," he said, revealing that he wondered sometimes if killing himself would be the only way to stop his pain. Then he started counseling through an organization in the Catholic Church. "It was a lifesaver to find out that I wasn't alone. Others were struggling, too, feeling rejected and hurt. I had a lot of growing and learning to do, " said this former electrical engineering professor.

In these meetings, he did, in truth, learn something very important—"what I was responsible for, and what I could change." Then, "it became obvious to me that it was time to go back to the Catholic Church. The more God became part of my life, the better my life became, " he said, adding this helped him reestablish a good relationship with his son, now 21.

His new connection with the Catholic Church got him an invitation to be part of the steering committee of the diocesan Family Life Office, and he became active in divorce ministry. In 1997 he was asked to be their representative at the North American Conference of Separated and Divorced Catholics meeting at Notre Dame. "I found the Conference to be wonderful. A great community gets built in a weekend. I was overwhelmed by the feeling of family, the closeness we felt."

Bob Dulinski came back to his home, and has worked for NACSDC ever since, because "This ministry does so much good. It's a wonderful thing for divorced Catholics. I wish we could get more bishops to see what we do at this Conference. Most people in the Church just don't know how spiritual, vibrant and important this ministry of separated and divorced Catholics is, and how much it is needed considering the divorce rate among Catholics."

Since my first contact with Irene Varley, I have spoken many times to her about the work being done by separated and divorced Catholics who want so honestly to remain connected to the Church. She describes the basic purpose of NACSDC is "to get the message across that despite divorce or separation, you are still a holy person. Too often people who have experienced the pain of divorce have felt the church was directed only towards families, and that they were no longer family. Indeed, they are still family, still holy, still very much a part of active parish participation."

In her own case, this mother of four affirms that her faith was strengthened after her divorce. "My marriage weakened my faith. In a bad marriage, you suffer a spiritual death that drains the soul because you become less aware of who you are. To keep and strengthen my faith, I knew that this—divorce—was what I had to do. So many people at the Conference tell us that they came back to the Church after their divorce. They gave up so much to keep the marriage going," she said, and all too often, this disconnected them from their faith.

Irene Varley has worked hard and long to help Catholics suffering from the negative effects of divorce and has made, she says, "a lot of discoveries," including a strengthened belief in how important it is for divorced Catholics to stay "connected to their faith." And she added that research shows where one stays in a close faith community, the likelihood of negatives from divorce is noticeably lessened.

There's a line that refers to "an idea whose time has come," and that would well apply to the founding of the North American Conference of Separated and Divorced Catholics in the mid-70s. Until that time, it was common to hear a statement emphasizing that "Good Catholics don't get divorced." Yet, that belief was far from the reality.

Yet, "So great was the power of that statement that thousands of divorcing Catholics were left with what they believed was their only alternative—namely to slip quiet-ly out of the Church, convinced that there was no point in turning to what had once been their 'home' for support and practical assistance," stated Paula Ripple Comin, who worked with Father Jim Young at the Paulist Center in Boston. "While many may have asked themselves why the Christian community did not seem to care about their deep hurts, most were too hurt or too fearful of further rejection to approach those who might have offered pastoral care.

"With the growth of many other forms of self-help support groups in the late '60s and early '70s, some divorcing men and women throughout the United States and Canada began to ask why such groups were not possible within the Catholic Church," she explained, in writing a history of NACSDC.

At the request of divorced and separated Catholics, who were meeting with Father Young at the Paulist Center and who wanted sincerely to remain faithful members of the Church, a ministry for them was set up in 1973. It was very similar to the program we had set up at the Cenacle Convent in the diocese of Rockville Centre. That same year, members organized a day-long conference for separated and divorced Catholics in Boston. This story got reported in newspapers around the country and even in *Time* magazine. Because of this attention, the Boston group came to be an information center where other such groups that had been forming throughout the country could network and share experiences. It was a surprise for us who had started the ministry for divorced and separated Catholics on Long Island to learn that similar groups existed in Portland, Seattle, Newark, Baltimore, and Minneapolis, besides other places we had not yet heard about.

There's a saying that nothing gallops like "an idea whose time has come," and that's what had happened. Within a year, "at the invitation of the Boston group, representatives from all the known support groups from the United States and Canada were invited to attend the second conference. From this meeting, "the framework for NACSDC was established," wrote Paula Ripple Comin. These founding members, announcing a conference in the Fall of 1975 at the University of Notre Dame, "met with representatives from their respective regions in order to begin to clarify the basic framework of the organization and to spell out the responsibilities of those who would, in later years, accept the leadership roles for NACSDC. Enthusiasm was high and heretofore unknown hope for divorcing Catholics spread rapidly on this continent," she affirmed.

Within the next decade—"Nudges from enthused and informed laity prompted bishops to write pastoral letters about the long overdue and much needed ministry to divorced and separated Catholics, and to participate in special 'homecoming' Masses and programs for those who felt 'unchurched,' alienated, excommunicated or unwanted," stated Kathleen L. Kircher, former Executive Director of NACSDC. The growth of the ministry was phenomenal, as, along with publications, workshops and local conferences becoming available, NACSDC was also able to counsel organizations and church agencies on strategies for giving pastoral care to the divorcing family.

"It was our hope that if the parish could become a wel-coming and nurturing place for Catholics undergoing divorce, more and more persons would truly become rec-onciled to the Church," in the words of Kathleen L. Kircher.

Her very statement subtly indicates what I too often heard from first-person tales, that going to the parish pas-tor with a need involving marriage could sometimes be a negative experience. As for how a parish priest treats a man or a woman in a troubled marriage coming to him for advice and help depends on how he sees himself, said Rev. Msgr. Dennis Regan, the former rector of the semi-nary in the Rockville Centre Diocese and now pastor of St. Rosalie's in Hampton Bays. And he underscored what he meant—"Am I a representative of a bureaucratic Church —or Christ?"

"My first response is to give them a warm welcome, lis-ten to their story and not jump in right off the bat. You have to know that you're talking to a person who values the Church, and has faith and confidence that the priest is there for them. That's a very good thing today. It says a lot already.

"Then, I try to relax them," Father Regan went on. "I tell them a lot of things happen in life that don't work out according to our expectations. But never forget—God is on your side. I want to reassure them they will be credibly listened to. You never know what they're thinking, but you can be confident that they came to see a priest believ-ing he is someone interested in their well-being."

Father Regan said, rather sadly, "Obviously, there are some situations where a person should not even have to return to their home that day. Some cases need more professional mediation than I can give. My counseling is from practical knowledge," said Father Regan, who is a moral theologian with expertise in medical ethics. But along with giving all the practical help he, as a pastor, can, he underscored, "You always emphasize their goodness, and God's love—and then take it from there."

A parish priest who asked not to be named said he takes pastoral responsibility very seriously, and believes, as the Church teaches, that in a true marriage, the two people living the marriage are blessed and bring their goodness to the world. But, he believes that since Vatican II the Church has made a special effort not only to uphold the indissolubility of Christian marriage, but also to teach clearly what marriage takes—"building material—persons who are psychologically capable to build new life together as a family, in partnership with God." He says he has no problem telling a couple that they need some heavy-duty marriage preparation classes if he determines they don't understand what Christian marriage means. "And that goes for someone who has had an annulment and now wants to remarry as well as first-timers," he emphasized.

Almost always, when divorced Catholics, who have made a decision to get remarried go to a priest, the annulment question does comes up. What is still often hard for them to understand is that a failed marriage is not necessarily an invalid one, and therefore an annulment is not automatically granted. They will be told there is help, for almost all dioceses have a Marriage Tribunal, staffed with psychologists, therapists and often volunteer advocates who assist divorced people seeking remarriage in the Church. There the emphasis is never focused on placing blame on one or the other.

"We are here to help," said Deacon Thomas Rich, one of the tribunal judges in the Diocese of Rockville Centre, in a story reported in *The Long Island Catholic*. He calls this work "a ministry," but immediately explains that what "needs to be proved" is that there were prior conditions that made it impossible to have an "indissoluble bond" with another, and therefore prevented a valid marriage. In Rockville Center, the Diocesan Office of Laity and Family periodically sponsors Annulment Information Nights to explain how the annulment process works and to clarify "myths and misconceptions" about it, said Deacon Rich.

Having to deal with annulment "myths" finally got to Father Juan-Diego Brunetta, a canon lawyer who serves on the Metropolitan Tribunal in Hartford, Connecticut. Mentioning all the calls they get exhibiting "a good deal of confusion about the very basics" of annulments, he wrote a clarification for *The Catholic Transcript*, the diocesan paper for the Hartford Archdiocese. The article had a very clear title: "Busting Some Common Annulment Myths."

He listed these myths as follows: (1) that a Declaration of Invalidity of Marriage is a reward that a spouse deserves because of one's long suffering in the marriage, etc. when it is, in actuality, granted because it was determined there was the presence of a serious obstacle to the marital bond at the time of the exchange of the vows; (2) that, for the spouse who is not seeking an annulment, it is a punishment or an accusation of wrongdoing by the other; (3) that annulment is "a sure thing;" (4) that a Declaration of Invalidity makes the children born of the marriage illegitimate; and (5) that an annulment is granted because of personal or financial influence.

Father Brunetta concluded his commentary, writing, that " . . . the annulment myths? They're Busted!" I smiled, appreciating not only the clarity of his piece, but his humor, too.

In my decades of concern for divorced and separated Catholics, I have seen that we have not been alone when it comes to wanting to underscore God's love over law in difficult marriage situations. My long time friend, Father John Catoir, former Director of the Christophers, known to many for his great interviews on the syndicated TV show "Christopher Closeups," has long expressed a pastoral concern for "the dilemma of divorced Catholics."

"We are dealing with mystery," he wrote nearly forty years ago. "The sacrament is not something that comes into existence by virtue of a legal presumption."

When I asked him in preparing this book how it was that he became so vocal in his concern for divorced and separated Catholics back in the late '60s, he answered honestly: "I had a doctorate in canon law and was the chief judge of the Marriage Tribunal in my diocese, Paterson, New Jersey. Many theologians—called 'the young Turks' back then—were calling for reform in the law which was very restrictive. I was one of them."

The basic belief in the late sixties when a Catholic couple sought a divorce was "you made your bed, now lie in it. The injustice of the law was that it denied the reality that people were living in. I never manipulated the law, but we had to consider the new knowledge we had received in the field of psychology," which so often pointed out that some people didn't have the capacity to enter into a valid, lifelong marriage.

"Lawyers, whether civil or ecclesiastical, are not competent to investigate the psychological factors concerned with the complexity of human love. The mystery of any human relationship so totally shatters the framework of the external juridical order that a lawyer or judge must be very humble before the mystery if he is to serve the total truth of the situation," said Father Catoir.

The day I was speaking with Father Catoir, January 30, 2006, a report had come from the Vatican that was headlined in the press as "Pope Appeals for 'Rapid' Rulings on Annulments." I was able to get further information from the Vatican, reported by Cindy Wooden of Catholic News Service. Pope Benedict XVI, meeting with members of the Roman Rota, a church court dealing mainly with marriage cases, had told them that for the good of individuals and the Catholic Church as a whole, marriage tribunals must act as quickly as possible while fully following Church law.

The purpose of an annulment procedure "is not to uselessly complicate the lives of the faithful nor even less to exacerbate litigiousness, but only to serve the truth," the Pope said. He pointed out that at times, it can appear that pastoral concern for people in irregular marriage situations clashes head-on with the Church's insistence that matrimony is forever and that annulment may be granted only when there is clear proof that the conditions for a valid marriage did not exist from the beginning.

But, the pope said, "The fundamental point of encounter between law and pastoral concern is love for the truth," and the pastoral value of an annulment— which allows remarried divorced Catholics to receive Communion—"cannot be separated from love for the truth."

At the same time, the pope underscored, the search for truth in a marriage case is very concrete and has a deep impact on the individuals involved. Because it touches both their human and Christian development, "it is very important that the declaration [of annulment] arrive in a reasonable amount of time ."

"Pope Benedict said it was also very important that the Church's pastoral approach to couples be evident long before any troubles arise. From the moment a couple requests to be married in a Catholic Church, he said priests must work to ensure that the couple understands the meaning of the sacrament of matrimony," Cindy Wooden reported.

Asking Father Catoir to comment on this very pastoral report, he said, "My take on this is that it is a good sign— characteristic of his general trend to be kind and just to people."

I had felt the same, and I base this on the fact that I had the enormous good fortune to meet our pope, then Cardinal Ratzinger, at a high level Conference for Christians and Jews held in Israel in February 1994. I had gotten an invitation to that conference because of my position as a syndicated columnist for Catholic News Service and the organizers hoped to get coverage in the Catholic press. The word was that this would be the largest assembly of high-level Christian and Jewish religious and educational leaders from around the world ever to come together in Israel.

Cardinal Ratzinger was there to represent Pope John Paul II. He gave a talk that reaffirmed the importance of Christian-Jewish relationships and then got personal, saying: "As a child . . . I could not understand how some people wanted to derive a condemnation of Jews from the death of Jesus." This was a German-born man speaking, one who in his youth had been conscripted into the Hitler Youth.

I cherish that day, when I had shaken his hand, been moved by his gentle, almost radiant smile and had even managed to get a photo of him on my little camera. When I heard he was chosen to be our pope, I was joyful, and hopeful that his true humanity will be felt by all. My Catholic faith was strengthened even more that day.

What I have learned in my decades of being a divorced Catholic and single parent is that the concern of my brothers and sisters who share my faith has been unbelievable healing balm poured over me, even if we never met in person. I remember the way the late Cardinal John O'Connor of New York reached out to single parents, supporting programs for them because he saw their "need for God and support from the Church."

Cardinal O'Connor encouraged parishes to have faith-based programs for parents who were single because of the death of a spouse, divorce, separation or conception of a child outside of marriage. A *Catholic New York* photo story in December 1998 told of the first "day of recollection" for single parents to be held in this diocese that drew over 75 mothers, fathers and children. The cardinal offered Mass and then met with and spoke warmly to these single parents, admitting he was aware that many single parents do not feel welcome and accepted in their parishes, and that some feel alienated from the Church because of the stigma attached to being divorced or separated or having a child born out of wedlock.

Going on, the cardinal acknowledged that "all single parents experience a profound loneliness and feeling of frustration associated with the difficulties of rearing children alone and meeting often inexorable demands on time and finances." And then he gave them real comfort when he said, "I am not here to judge or lecture you. I am here to help and to offer whatever help the Church can give."

At this time, I had been asked to give a talk on divorce and remarriage, with many pushing me on why I believed so deeply in the importance of receiving the Eucharist. I didn't have to come up with a personal answer. I was able to give them what I believe is the "universal" answer, so well explained by the cardinal in that talk to single parents. He said: "Unless we *remind ourselves that God loves us*, we have nothing in our lives that we can count on. This is why the Mass has to become so meaningful, why the reception of Holy Communion has to become so meaningful. In this sacrament we truly experience the fact that God loves me for myself." And he urged all who were there to allow themselves to be "transformed into Christ" when they receive Communion, promising them, "You will see wonders you never saw before in your children and in yourselves."

That's the bottom-line message; that's why we want to stay connected to our Church. I have remained ever grateful to priests—and a cardinal—who were so Christ-like in helping their divorced and separated brothers and sisters see and believe that we have never been abandoned by our loving Lord.

I have also remained personally ever grateful to the many divorced and separated Catholics who have contacted me over the years, either asking for my advice or my prayers. Sometimes, sadly, they would tell me they had been "cut off" from the Church and now it no longer mattered to them. Then others would simply say a thank you that I have never lost my "vote of confidence" in myself or them, that we would stay faithful to our families and our faith.

Perhaps no letter ever moved me as much as the one I received in 1996 from a woman I didn't know named Agnes Brien, who was then the assistant city clerk of the city of Norwalk, Connecticut. I was at that time the executive editor of *The Litchfield County Times*, a secular weekly in Connecticut. The paper was sent to major offices in many cities and towns, including Norwalk, and Agnes recognized my name. She wrote me a letter, beginning with a sentence that somewhat shocked me. She said that back in the late '70s, I had "saved her life."

The explanation Agnes gave moved me deeply. She explained that she had been left with a broken marriage and seven children to raise, one of them hardly more than a baby. She had been feeling sorry for herself, defeated and almost despairing. Somehow, she came across a book I had just written, *A Parent Alone*, in which I shared my story of being a single mother left to raise a large family. The book inspired her, she wrote. She felt if I could make a life for myself and my seven children—still hanging on to my Catholic faith—so could she. She found a job and a way to get the younger children cared for, and she took some courses, getting enough credentials to qualify her for the assistant city clerk job, working directly with the mayor.

I was deeply touched, and I called Agnes right away. It was as though we were instant sisters. We arranged to meet at a restaurant half way between our two locations. I discovered I had met a woman of deep faith, who had been part of the Cursillo movement, and the charismatic renewal, crediting both for helping in her faith journey. We became friends forever.

Soon after, Agnes retired from her job and worked for several volunteer Christian programs. Now, even our heartfelt work runs the same course, both of us believing in the need for peace and justice in our world, with special pro-life concerns, including following the teachings of the Catholic bishops on working to end the death penalty in our nation. I don't think it was by coincidence that Agnes read my book back in 1978 and remembered it, that she wrote to me and we met. I think it was just another of the graces God gives to us, to bring people into our lives who have a nobility that can be shared with us.

I have heard so many stories, met so many good people baptized into the Catholic community, who have never given up on their faith, even though they have lived or are still living difficult lives. They are my comfort and my inspiration. Yet, on the other hand, I have so often been challenged by people who have given up on God because of their lost or shattered dreams of happiness. And all I can tell them is what I have learned—that God never gives up on us. St. Augustine assures us:

> *There are days when the burdens we carry chafe our shoulders and wear us down,*
>> *When the road seems dreary and endless, the skies grey and threatening;*
> *When our lives have no music in them and our hearts are lonely,*
>> *And our souls have lost their courage.*
> *Flood the path with light, we beseech Thee, O Lord,*
>> *Turn our eyes—to where the heavens are full of promise!*

Questions for Reflection and Discussion

1. What new resources did you discover you had during your transition from married to single life?
2. Did you go to your diocesan Marriage Tribunal for information and assistance, and if so, how were you received?
3. If you went for an annulment, what was your experience, and how would you advise someone to proceed, based on what you learned?

Hopeful Thoughts—from
My Heart to Yours

IF I were to be asked what I feel is still needed when it comes to the subject of why some Catholic marriages fail my answer would be simply, "Do not judge." No one really knows what has gone on behind closed doors, or what resources one has been given to deal with whatever happens.

There never was a guarantee that we, though baptized in the love of the Lord Jesus Christ, would be spared searing pain in our lives. On the contrary, sometimes I have suspected that we are the new "chosen ones," selected to live as our founder did, faithful to the death. I confess I have felt that way, deeply, when I finally had to acknowledge that there was no true love or fidelity in my marriage; and then later, when my youngest son Peter, battling a mental illness, died after putting a gun to his head, and my son John and his wife Nancy died after an 18-year-old killer put a gun to their heads, and my adopted son Sterling died after a heart and kidney transplant failed.

I have screamed at God, and yet, always, his Son was nearby to dry my tears and let me know that so long as I didn't give up on him, he would always be there as he promised: "I will not leave you orphaned; I am coming to you." As for how—by giving us the most amazing, enduring miracle imaginable: Food, his own body and blood, to keep us alive forever. That's why we, baptized in his life, are the Lord's new chosen ones, not only to the death, but to the Resurrection and Life Eternal.

That's not to say I have never doubted these Gospel messages, or never found myself tongue-tied at times when trying to explain to non-believers the mystery of the Eucharist. It's just that if I thought of living a day, with unresolved doubts about the truth of Jesus, I would truly fall into despair. That knocks me to my knees, and then, gratefully, *he* picks me up.

I have to go back to third grade when I am asked why I believe so deeply in the Eucharist. It was a religion lesson in class at the Blessed Sacrament Church in my hometown of Albany, N.Y. and our teacher, Sister Mary Edwin, started talking about Holy Communion. She wasn't using a catechism or a book. She was addressing us directly in words like this: Every time you receive Holy Communion, Jesus' body and blood, that's real food. And just like real food, it becomes part of your own body and blood.

Then Sister slightly rolled up her sleeves, and gesturing, told us to look at her hands. She went on to talk about how the cells of these hands contained Jesus, and I remember how she went on about how important our bodies were because our very molecules were formed with the body of Christ Jesus. I started looking at my own hands. I had never before thought of Communion as being a bodily nourishment, only something we took for the soul.

I don't know if any of my young classmates were impressed, as I was, by Sister Mary Edwin's simple, but logical, sense of how we are *physically* part of God because of Holy Communion, but she had given me a lesson to remember for life. I had often trudged to morning Mass, beginning at age 7, but after that lesson, I made daily Mass a practice, and rarely missed a morning until after I was married.

I think it was mostly because I felt so strongly about the necessity of the Eucharist in our lives that I did want to work in the ministry for divorced and separated Catholics back in the early '70s, when annulments were still misunderstood. One of the saddest stories that came up too often was how a wife or husband in pain would get no understanding from their pastor. I'm sure all of us who are divorced or separated can remember an unpleasant, or even cruel, encounter we had where someone judged us unfairly and/or unpleasantly. I will never forget when I was the editor of a secular newspaper, the pastor of a Catholic Church wanted some publicity and I agreed to go to the rectory to interview him. Once there, he offered to take me to lunch, if I would drive him and his dog to the restaurant. I did.

Part way through the lunch, when we had briefly talked about my children, he asked me what my husband did for a living. I told him I was divorced. At that, he looked at me with disgust and said, "If I had known you were divorced, I would never have invited you to lunch."

This priest has been deceased for a number of years, but I still pray that he had softened his heart before going to meet the compassionate Lord Jesus. The postscript to this story is that at the beginning of this year of 2006, this parish began a program of support for divorced and separated Catholics. God does arrange for his healing work!

There still needs to be much more understanding about difficult marriages, and all the ways suffering can be inflicted by one or another, or both, in a marriage. I worked with battered women in my younger years, and heard of marriages that were horror stories because of physical abuse triggered by alcohol, psychological illness, or the need to assert power and authority. I listened to Catholic women tearfully telling me how a priest had said a beating was not grounds for divorce; it wasn't adultery. And I met some Catholic men, too, in painful marriages, like one who told me, actually with a smile, that he was "not the abuser, but the abused!"

I knew they were speaking the truth for I, too, had been told over and over in the late '50s and early '60s that I had to stay in my marriage, because this was "God's plan" for my salvation and my husband's salvation. At that time, I never challenged what a priest told me, though I would always wonder how I got to be responsible for my husband's soul, especially considering that he had studied to be a Jesuit priest for nine years! But I always controlled my anger, believing a line I had read: "Speak when you are angry and you will make the best speech you will ever regret."

When I gave talks after my single parenting book came out, I would try to be as upbeat as possible. At one of these, a woman who had obviously emerged into a healed state after divorce had come in holding a banner saying, "Tomorrow Is Another Day." Another woman, newly divorced, looked at her, read the words aloud and added, "Yeah, that's what I'm afraid of!"

Understandably—because here's the deal: After divorce, we're coping with altered relationships, with everybody. We have a new fear of the future, where everything we had hoped for and planned for is completely altered. We struggle not to let ourselves develop a "failure" image. We're not sure of our rights, or of our abilities now that we are in a completely new situation. We need to rebuild our self-image. Our personal life needs to be redirected, and this means we must try to find a focus outside ourselves, something that interests us, or better yet, excites us. We have to watch that the most self-destructive trap of all doesn't lock us in, and I'm talking of self-pity and depression.

After a divorce, there is a loss of intimacy that too often catapults one into a new kind of loneliness—the utter sense of disconnection with everything. You feel that if you took a walk, baked a cake, sang a song, cried or smiled, no one would really see you, no one would really care. This is a time of darkness when one really needs to turn to God, who is the only one who can help us find our wholeness again.

"Divorce is the cause of so much pain," writes Father John Catoir in his beautiful book titled *Joy, The Spirit's Gigantic Secret Behind the Church's Survival.* "If only two former lovers could return to the joy of their original attraction. Even so, divorces do occur and usually for good reason. We try to encourage the victims of divorce; they are not poor, helpless creatures, there is always grace. There can be life after divorce, and even divine Joy in the knowledge of God's love. Those who cling to God in their misery can find their way back to some kind of normalcy," he affirms.

I certainly found that to be true in my own life. A traumatic experience like divorce or death shocks a person to the core. As such, it has the potential of destroying one's spiritual growth, if you choose to stay locked in a spiritual immobility. Or, it can bring you to a rebirth, releasing a new spiritual energy which leads to personal harmony and peace. As a friend once told me, "I feel a person must first discard the negative state of mind before any success will come. When things get bad enough, one does just that. . . . I finally turned to Jesus. It took me four years, but I did it. I put aside my burdens, turned to him, and responded to his touch. I haven't let go since . . ."

If I feel a sadness these days, it is in the statistics I read that show a growing disconnection to the Church on the part of many Catholics. A book published in late 2005, titled *Catholicism in Motion, the Church in American Society* by James D. Davidson, gives statistics that, I believe, need attention:

- The percentage of Catholics attending Mass each week now is about half of what it was fifty years ago.
- The trend toward interfaith marriage continues—29 percent of Catholics are involved in interfaith marriages.
- Catholics are increasingly marrying outside the Church—40 percent among post-Vatican II Catholics.
- Seventy-three percent of young women (versus 63 percent of young men) said one could be a good Catholic without agreeing with the Church's policies on divorce and remarriage. When asked if one could be a good Catholic without marrying in the Church, 73 percent of young women (versus 57 percent of young men) responded in the affirmative.

The author writes: "These results pose some serious challenges. We should be concerned that Catholics involved in both intrafaith (both Catholics) and interfaith (one non-Catholic) marriages increasingly are marrying outside the Church. If Church leaders have not done so already, they might look to see if this trend is occurring in their parishes and dioceses, investigate the reasons behind it, and consider ways to respond to it."

On the good-news side, the author has found that 63 percent of Catholics said belief that "the bread and wine actually become the Body and Blood of Christ" is very important to them. He said we "should be impressed by the fact that the vast majority of American Catholics—including young adults—put belief in the Real Presence at the very center of their personal faith. Catholic laypeople have their own hierarchy of truths and believing that the bread and wine are transformed into the Body and Blood of Christ is right up there at the top."

I have already shared why I so strongly believe in the Eucharist, its nourishment and power to sustain us in troubled times. As Father John Catoir emphasizes in his book on joy, "This sacrament makes theology a personal reality. The main reason that most Catholics have remained loyal to the Church down through time, in spite of their misgivings about the hierarchy and the scandals, is due to their faith in the Real Presence of Jesus Christ in the Eucharist. The Blessed Eucharist is called the 'Bread of Angels,' because it is true spiritual food worthy of the noblest being. This is a sacred gift, but you don't have to be an angel to receive it." I think Father wrote that last line with conviction and a smile.

I am so grateful that I have had the opportunity to share my belief, from the experiences of my life, that a failed Catholic marriage does not mean the erosion of our spiritual lives. On the contrary, if we can remember that we are rooted in grace—which the French poet Jacques Riviere so inspiringly defined as "God's footprints in our soul"—we can grow in faith. I leave you with an impressive confirmation of this, attributed to the late Canon John Andrew, when he was rector of St. Thomas Episcopal Church in New York:

"As to all who complain that God has somehow removed himself from their ability to reach him, I am always tempted to ask, 'Who moved?' "

That perhaps is the final question to ponder.

Resources

Annulment: A Step-by-Step Guide for Divorced Catholics, Smith, Rev. Ronald T., $9.95.

Healing the Wounds of Divorce, Stipp, Ruth and David, Abbey Press Care Notes, St. Meinrad, IN.

Healing the Wounds of Divorce: A Spiritual Guide to Recovery, Schlemon, Barbara Leahy, Ave Maria Press, $9.95.

Joy, The Spirit's Gigantic Secret Behind the Church's Survival, Catoir, Father John, Alba House, $14.95.

Prayers for Catholics Experiencing Divorce, Bedar, Vicki Wells and Rev. William Rabior, NACSDC, $4.95.

With Open Arms: Catholics, Divorce, and Remarriage, Hosie, John, Liguori, $3.95.

North American Conference of Separated and Divorced
Catholics, Inc. [NACSDC]
    P.O. Box 10
    Hancock, MI 49930
    906-482-0494
    e-mail: office@nacsdc.org
    web: www.nacsdc.org

ANTOINETTE BOSCO has written "The Bottom Line" for the Catholic News Service since 1974. She was formerly the executive editor of the *Litchfield County Times* and wrote for *The Long Island Catholic* for eleven years. She served on the Suffolk County, Long Island Human Rights Commission and was a faculty and staff member at State University of New York at Stony Brook. She has written more than 250 magazine articles and was honored in 2002 with a Christopher award and a Pax Christi award for *Choosing Mercy, A Mother of Murder Victims Pleads to End the Death Penalty,* which also received wide critical acclaim. In September 2005 she was honored with the National Council of Catholic Women's Distinguished Service Award. *Growing in Faith When a Catholic Marriage Fails* is her fourteenth book. A single mother of seven, three deceased, she lives in Brookfield, Connecticut.

OTHER BOOKS OF INTEREST

SOMETIMES I HAVEN'T GOT A PRAYER
... And Other "Real" Catholic Adventures
Mary Kavanagh Sherry

". . . down-to-earth, even extremely funny, and filled with insights born of love and lighthearted determination to be a growing yet faithful believer committed to Catholicism."
—Dominican Vision

No. RP 174/04 ISBN 1-878718-79-7   **$8.95**

THE POWER OF ONE
Christian Living in the Third Millennium
Msgr. Jim Lisante

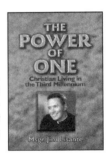

"Many of the stories could be used in counselling sessions, religious education classes, or Bible studies as explorations of love, compassion, anger, frustration and caring. The stories are short but have deep meaning." **—Crux of the News**

No. RP 180/04 ISBN 1-878718-84-3   **$9.95**

LOVING YOURSELF FOR GOD'S SAKE
Adolfo Quezada

This exquisite book of meditations gently directs the reader to see the gift of self in an entirely new and beautiful light. It presents a spirituality of self-love not based on narcissism, but as a response to the divine invitation to self-nurturing.

No. RP 720/04 ISBN 1-878718-35-5   **$5.95**

A PARTY OF ONE
Meditations for Those Who Live Alone
Joni Woelfel

Using each day's brief reflection, probing question and pertinent quote by Adolfo Quezada, this book will comfort and empower those living alone to take ownership of their life, confident of being guided and upheld by God.

No. RP 744/04 ISBN 1-933066-01-6   **$5.95**

OTHER BOOKS OF INTEREST

LIFE, LOVE AND LAUGHTER
The Spirituality of the Consciousness Examen
Father Jim Vlaun

"Within only a few pages, you know you're in the company of a truly good man, someone with a big heart whose feet are firmly on the ground . . . There is so much simple, shining wisdom in this book." —*William J,. O'Malley, S.J.*

No. RP 113/04 ISBN 1-878718-43-6   **$7.95**

HEART PEACE
Embracing Life's Adversities
Adolfo Quezada

"This is one of the most authentic books I have ever read on the gut-wrenching conditions that cause or lead to human suffering. . . . His book is a gift, allowing others to be the beneficiaries of his spiritual journey." —*Antoinette Bosco*

No. RP 117/04 ISBN 1-878718-52-5   **$9.95**

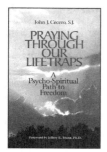

PRAYING THROUGH OUR LIFETRAPS
A Psycho-Spiritual Path to Freedom
John J. Cecero, S.J.

"John Cecero's unique book can be read not only as a primer on lifetrap therapy and practice but as a spiritual guide to finding God in all things."

—*Joseph R. Novello, M.D.*

No. RP 164/04 ISBN 1-878718-70-3   **$9.95**

GRACE NOTES
Embracing the Joy of Christ in a Broken World
Lorraine V. Murray

". . . will help you to see what we should be able to see naturally, but for some reason it takes grace to recognize grace! Her book is well named."

—*Fr. Richard Rohr, O.F.M.*

No. RP 154/04 ISBN 1-878718-69-X   **$9.95**

Additional Titles Published by Resurrection Press, a Catholic Book Publishing Imprint

For a free catalog call 1-800-892-6657
www.catholicbookpublishing.com